A First Guide to
Birdwatching

A First Guide to Birdwatching

Chris Harbard

Oxford University Press

A QUARTO BOOK

Published by
Oxford University Press, Walton Street, Oxford, OX2 6DP

Oxford New York Toronto
Delhi Bombay Calcutta Madras Karachi
Kuala Lumpur Singapore Hong Kong Tokyo Nairobi
Dar es Salaam Cape Town
Melbourne Auckland Madrid

and associate companies in Berlin Ibadan

Oxford is a trade mark of Oxford University Press

Copyright © 1993 Quarto Children's Books Ltd

All rights reserved. No part of this publication may be reproduced, stored in a retrieval system, or transmitted, in any form or by any means, without the prior permission in writing of Oxford University Press. Within the UK, exceptions are allowed in respect of any fair dealing for the purpose of research or private study, or criticism or review, as permitted under the Copyright, Designs and Patents Act, 1988, or in the case of reprographic reproduction in accordance with the terms of the licences issued by the Copyright Licensing Agency. Enquiries concerning reproduction outside these terms and in other countries should be sent to the Rights Department, Oxford University Press, at the address above.

This book is sold subject to the condition that it shall not, by way of trade or otherwise, be lent, re-sold, hired out or otherwise circulated without the publisher's prior consent in any form of binding or cover other than that in which it is published and without a similar condition including this condition being imposed on the subsequent purchaser.

A CIP catalogue record for this book is available from the British Library.

ISBN 0 19 910059 4

This book was designed and produced by
Quarto Children's Books Ltd
The Old Brewery 6 Blundell Street London N7 9BH

Creative Director Nick Buzzard
Managing Editor Christine Hatt
Editor Beverly LeBlanc
Designer Rebecca Herringshaw
Illustrators Wayne Ford, David Kerr, Paul Richardson
Picture Manager Dipika Parmar-Jenkins

The Publishers would like to thank the following for their help in the preparation of this book: Janette Earney, Alan Mole

Picture Acknowledgements
Key: a = above, b = below, l = left, r = right, c = centre
Quarto Publishing would like to thank the following for supplying photographs and for permission to reproduce copyright material. While every effort has been made to trace and acknowledge all copyright holders, we would like to apologize should any omissions have been made.

Robert Dickson/Natural Image, page 54cr. C. Downey/RSPB, pages 13br, 13b, 82bl. Bob Gibbons/Natural Image, pages 23a, 23cr, 55a, 80bl. J. Hollis/Aquila, page 40cr. C H. Gomersall/RSPB, pages 10b, 11br, 12a, 13ar, 15ar, 20bl, 54al, 68a, 70c. Mike Lane/Natural Image, pages 17b, 56cl, 69al. J. Markham/RSPB, page 13c. George McCarthy, pages 10al, 18b, 22bl, 25b, 57br, 71cr, 81a. Richard T. Mills/Aquila, pages 19a, 21c. T. Nottingham/Natural Image, page 71b. R. Revels/RSPB, page 13bl. Roger Reynolds/Trip, pages 19cl, 21br, 25ar, 31ar, 82cl. Michael W. Richards/RSPB, pages 57ar, 82al. RSPB, pages 29a, 30a, 30c, 30b, 40cl, 42c. William S. Paton, pages 23c, 83a. Roger Tidman/Nature Photographers Ltd, pages 24bl, 43cr, 55ar. Bob Turner/Trip, pages 28a. Roger Wilmshurst/Trip, pages 20b, 21cr/RSPB, pages 21cl, 41cr, 42c, 56al, 57al. Peter Wilson/Natural Image, pages 22c, 42b. Michael J. Woods/Natural Image, page 24br. Mike Wilkes/Aquila, page 43ar.

Front jacket photographs supplied by: Toby Schmidt/Running Press – centre, George McCarthy above.
Back jacket photograph supplied by: Robert Dickson/Natural Image – above, C. H. Gomersall/RSPB – bottom.

Typeset by Central Southern Typesetters, Eastbourne, Sussex
Manufactured in Hong Kong by Regent Publishing Services Ltd
Printed by Leefung-Asco Printers Ltd, Hong Kong

Contents

Birds and Birdwatching 10
Bird Bodies **16**
Bird Behaviour **20**
Bird Life Cycles **22**
Migration **24**

Bird Profiles 26

Town and Garden Birds 28

Woodland Birds 40

Open Country and Upland Birds 54

River, Lake, and Marsh Birds 68

Coast and Estuary Birds 80

Glossary 90

Index 92

Birds and Birdwatching

▼ Pretty Profile
The first clue to identifying a bird may be its profile, as in the long necks of these Canada geese.

The greatest attraction of birdwatching is that it can be enjoyed anywhere at almost any time. From city parks and suburban gardens to coastal estuaries or upland moors, birds are everywhere.

Birdwatching is easy to begin. All you have to do is look. Start by becoming familiar with the common birds around you and gradually build up the number of birds you recognize. Seeing a bird may be easy, but identifying it can often be difficult. The ideal way to learn more is to go out with a knowledgeable birdwatcher. Join a birdwatching club or Young Ornithologists' Club group (see address on page 91) which has regular outings and welcomes newcomers.

Beginners often find the variety of birds bewildering. But be patient. What is difficult at first soon becomes second nature as increasing numbers of new birds become familiar.

▶ Look and Learn
Many birds survive by eating plants, as well as the insects that live on them. If you learn which plants birds eat, you will have another identification clue. Here, an instructor examines cow parsley with young birdwatchers. Birds do not eat cow parsley, but the flies which it attracts.

BIRDS AND BIRDWATCHING

DIFFERENT SHAPES

Birds come in many different shapes. Use a bird's shape to help you tell what it is, or to distinguish between two similar species. Look for clues like tail length, shape of wings, and length of legs or neck.

▲ **Starling or Blackbird?**
Blackbirds have more rounded wings than starlings and a longer tail.

▲ **Great Tit or Long-tailed Tit?**
Great tits have short, rounded wings and small heads. Long-tailed tits have rounded bodies and, as their name suggests, very long tails.

▲ **Swift or Swallow?**
Swifts have long, pointed wings and a short, notched tail. Swallows have a longer, forked tail and shorter wings.

◀ **Canada Goose or Mallard?**
Canada geese have longer wings and necks than mallards and their tails look shorter.

◀ **Chaffinch or Pied Wagtail?**
Chaffinches have notched tails and rounded wings. Pied wagtails have longer, square-ended tails.

▼ **Look Up**
All you have to do to start birdwatching is open your eyes and look up. The sky is filled with a fascinating variety of birds. Looking through a pair of binoculars helps you see details on the birds more clearly, but they are not an essential piece of equipment. You can have fun birdwatching without them!

WHEN TO BIRDWATCH

Early morning is probably the best time to watch birds, as they usually go looking for food just after they have woken up. In spring it is also the best time to listen to them, because this is when you will hear all the birds singing together in the dawn chorus. Birds are generally quieter later in the day, becoming more active again before dusk.

Any time of the year is good for birdwatching. Many male birds are brightly coloured in spring and sing loudly as they try to attract a mate. Birds become more quiet during the

BIRDS AND BIRDWATCHING

BEST BIRD-WATCHING BEHAVIOUR

- ALWAYS put the welfare of the bird first.
- DO NOT go too close to a nest which is being used.
- BE quiet and patient.
- NEVER take birds' eggs, even from old nests.
- DO NOT go onto private land without permission.
- STAY ON public footpaths.
- REMEMBER all wild birds and their nests and eggs are protected by law.

▶ **Lying Low**
Getting a good look at birds can take time and patience. Keep a low profile by hiding behind a natural screen such as a tree or a grass bank.

▼ **Better View**
A pair of binoculars can give a keen birdwatcher a much better view. To start with, a simple pair of 8 x 30 binoculars are best. They are not too heavy, but are still quite powerful. Always try out a pair before deciding which to buy, to make sure you feel comfortable using them.

Use the central wheel to focus on any birds you spot.

Always keep the strap around your neck so that you don't drop your binoculars.

A pair of light binoculars like this is ideal for the beginner.

breeding season in an attempt to draw less attention to their nests and eggs. But do look out for the arrival of the first summer visitors, like swallows. At the end of the summer birds lose many of their feathers. They hide away until their new feathers have grown.

In the autumn, the summer birds begin to leave for their winter homes further south and the first of the winter visitors start to arrive from their breeding grounds further north. Coastal areas are always worth visiting at this time of year, as many birds passing through from northern breeding areas can be seen.

Winter is a good time to see large numbers of birds that flock together outside the breeding season. Thousands of waders, ducks, geese, and swans can be found on coastal and inland wetlands. Redwings can be found along hedgerows and in fields. Many other birds take refuge on the warmer, ice-free water in gravel pits and reservoirs.

GETTING STARTED

Birds can easily be watched at close quarters in gardens and parks, but to see birds well elsewhere a pair of

BIRDS AND BIRDWATCHING

binoculars is necessary. This is the only expensive piece of equipment you will need to invest in unless you become a very serious birdwatcher.

When choosing binoculars, check the magnification first. This will tell you how much bigger birds and the surrounding scenery will appear when you look through the lenses. A pair of binoculars marked 8 × 30, for example, will magnify everything eight times and have lenses that are 30 millimetres across. A 10 × 50 pair will magnify everything ten times and have 50 millimetre lenses. Any binoculars with more than ten times magnification should be avoided, as they will not give you better views.

Telescopes are not essential but can be very useful when watching distant birds on a reservoir or estuary. They are, however, expensive and heavy to carry.

Photography and sound recording are popular activities often associated with birdwatching. But carrying cameras, lenses, or tape recorders, as well as binoculars, is not easy, so it is best not to mix these activities at first.

◀ **Home-Making**
The breeding season is a bird's busiest time. Once a nest site has been found, birds have to collect building materials.

A DAY IN THE LIFE

From dawn to dusk, birds are busy eating, sleeping, and keeping clean. In spring and summer they also build nests, attract mates, fight off rivals, and feed young. Luckily there are more hours of daylight at these times, and plenty of food. In winter, half the day is spent sleeping, so a warm, safe place to roost is vital.

▲ **Sweet Song**
In the breeding season, birds may spend the day in song.

◀ **Feeding Time**
Birds spend most of their lives feeding. In winter, nearly all the daylight hours can be spent looking for food. Some birds change their diet, feeding on insects in spring and summer, then switching to berries or seeds.

▶ **Feather Care**
Birds need clean feathers to keep warm and dry. After bathing, they preen their feathers, which cleans them and releases natural oils to waterproof them.

◀ **Resting Easy**
The place a bird chooses to sleep is called a roost. Dunlin roost together in flocks at high tide.

13

BIRDS AND BIRDWATCHING

CAREFUL OBSERVATIONS
Birdwatching is all about being patient and quiet. In woodland it is best to find a comfortable place to sit, with a good view all round, and wait for the birds to come past. Hides, provided at many nature reserves, are waterproof, hut-like structures that make birdwatching more comfortable. Birds do not realize people are inside, so it is important to be quiet.

Don't wear bright clothing for birdwatching, but choose colours that blend in with the surrounding countryside, so that birds don't notice you. Always wrap up warm in winter and wear a wind-proof coat with a hood or hat, and warm boots.

MAKING NOTES
Always take a notebook with you to make notes. These will help you identify a bird once you get home.

▼ **Quick ID**
Answering six very simple questions will give you a headstart in identifying any bird. Jot the questions listed below down in your notebook to remind you.

SIX STEPS TO BIRD IDENTIFICATION

1 WHAT SIZE IS IT?
This is probably the first thing you notice. To gauge a bird's size, compare it in your mind's eye with one you already know.

House sparrow, Blackbird, Woodpigeon, Pheasant, Mute swan

2 WHAT SHAPE IS IT?
Look at the lengths of the tail, beak, and legs. Is the beak thin, straight, or curved? Is the tail pointed or rounded?

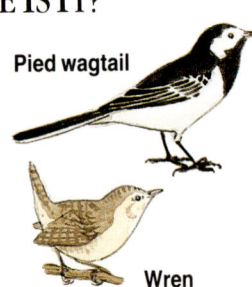

Pied wagtail, Wren

3 HOW DOES IT WALK?
The way a bird moves on the ground can give it away. Does it hop, like a jay, walk like a jackdaw, or run like a starling?

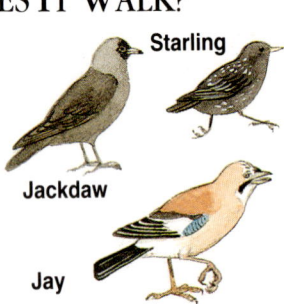

Starling, Jackdaw, Jay

4 WHERE DID YOU SEE IT?
Most birds prefer one type of habitat. You are most likely to see a dunlin on the coast, for instance.

5 HOW DOES IT FLY?
Some birds fly straight, while others 'bound' up and down. Some flocks fly straight, others prefer a V.

Cuckoo, Woodpecker

6 IS IT ALONE OR IN A GROUP?
Some birds, such as starlings, like to flock together, while others, like kestrels, are usually alone.

BIRDS AND BIRDWATCHING

Make your notes as soon as you see a bird. Checklists are useful for simply recording species seen but details of numbers, and whether birds are nesting or singing are useful information as well. Also, do not forget to write where and when you saw the birds. A note of the time of day, weather, temperature, and wind direction is also helpful.

It is important to name the parts of a bird correctly when you are making your notes. Watch a common bird like a house sparrow and get familiar with its feathers (see pages 16–19) and markings.

Even the most experienced birdwatchers take field guides with them. These contain illustrations of many birds, and descriptions of their appearance and habits. This book gives you all this information.

Keeping Notes

It is important to take accurate notes. A pocket looseleaf notebook is easiest to carry, and pencils are best because they don't run in wet weather. The most important facts to note are the species you see, where, when, and how many of them.

▲ **Glorious Goldfinch**
A perfect view of a goldfinch feeding in autumn. Its red face and yellow banded wings are clearly visible.

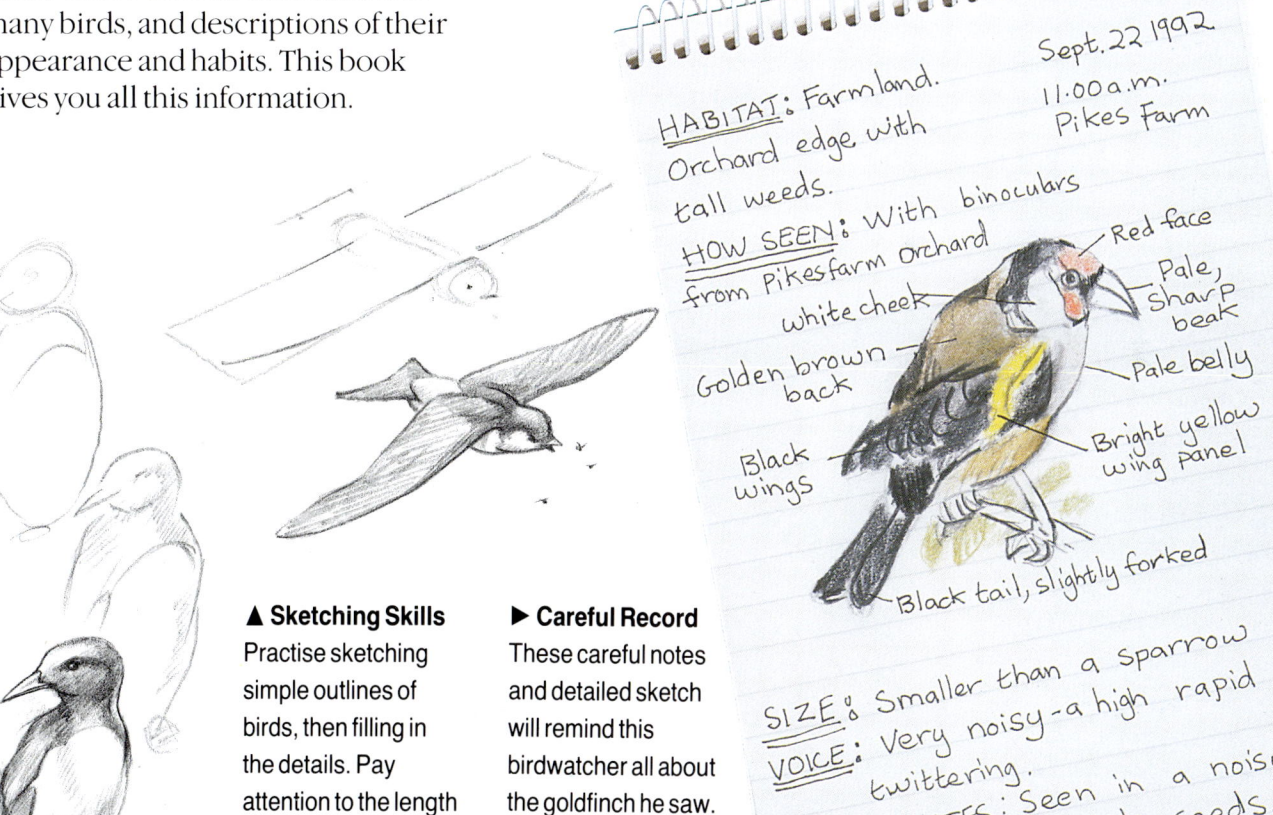

▲ **Sketching Skills**
Practise sketching simple outlines of birds, then filling in the details. Pay attention to the length of wings, tail, and beak. A quick, rough sketch is better than none at all, and will help you write up your records later.

▶ **Careful Record**
These careful notes and detailed sketch will remind this birdwatcher all about the goldfinch he saw. Notice how he considers all the information before deciding which species he has spotted.

BIRD BODIES

Once you start birdwatching you will quickly see how well birds are designed for their lifestyle. They have hollow bones that make them light, well-developed muscles specifically used for flying, and feathers on their wings that support them in the air. All birds have feathers, wings, tails, beaks, and feet. These different features provide the clues to identifying a species.

FLYING FEATHERS

Feathers give birds their ability to fly, and keep them dry and warm. They may also be decorative, forming crests or tail streamers. Their colours may be bright to attract a mate, or dull to hide and protect the bird from its enemies. It is usually the males of the species that are most colourful.

A birds' feathers grow out of its skin, like hair on humans. A typical wing or tail feather has a central shaft with broad vanes on either side (see box).

Smaller body feathers, called down feathers, have different barbs which do not lock together. They are very soft and grow next to the skin,

▼ **Wing Tips**
Wing feathers can help you identify a bird. Look for wing bars, which are formed by coloured tips on the wing coverts. Look out for white outer tail feathers, too. These will often help you distinguish species.

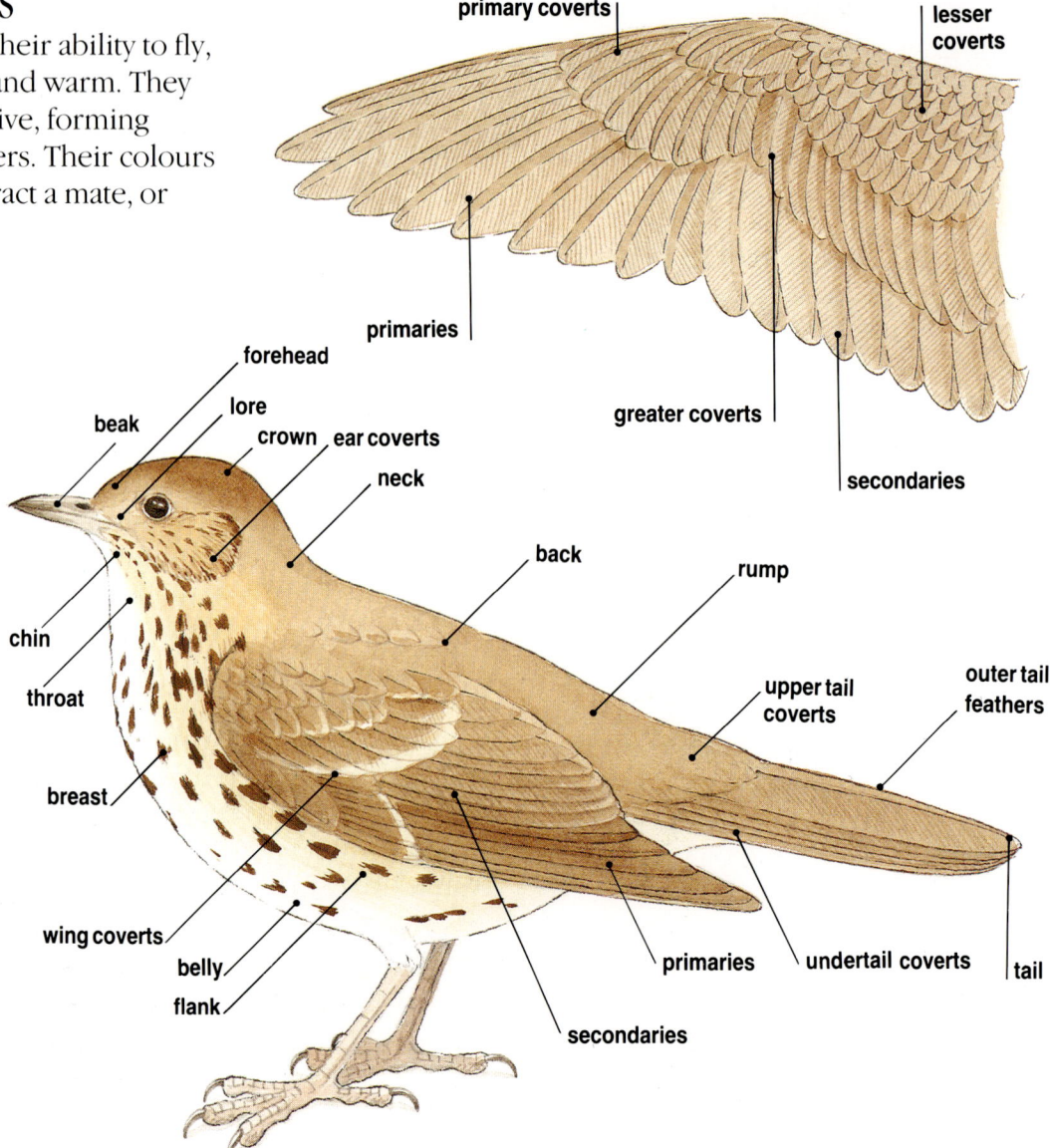

▶ **Naming the Parts**
Learning to name the different parts of a bird's plumage (feathers) will help you describe it accurately to other people, and to understand its description in a field guide. The upper parts of a bird start at the forehead and end at the upper tail coverts. The underparts begin with the chin and finish with the undertail coverts. The head is often difficult to describe – look for the lores and ear coverts and note any stripes through or above the eye.

covering the whole body of most adult birds. Down feathers trap air to provide waterproofing and insulation. They are easy to see on young birds, but are less visible on adults as they are hidden beneath the outer body feathers.

All birds' feathers gradually wear out and new ones grow in their place. This is a process called moulting, which usually occurs after the breeding season. The number of feathers on birds differs. Swans have

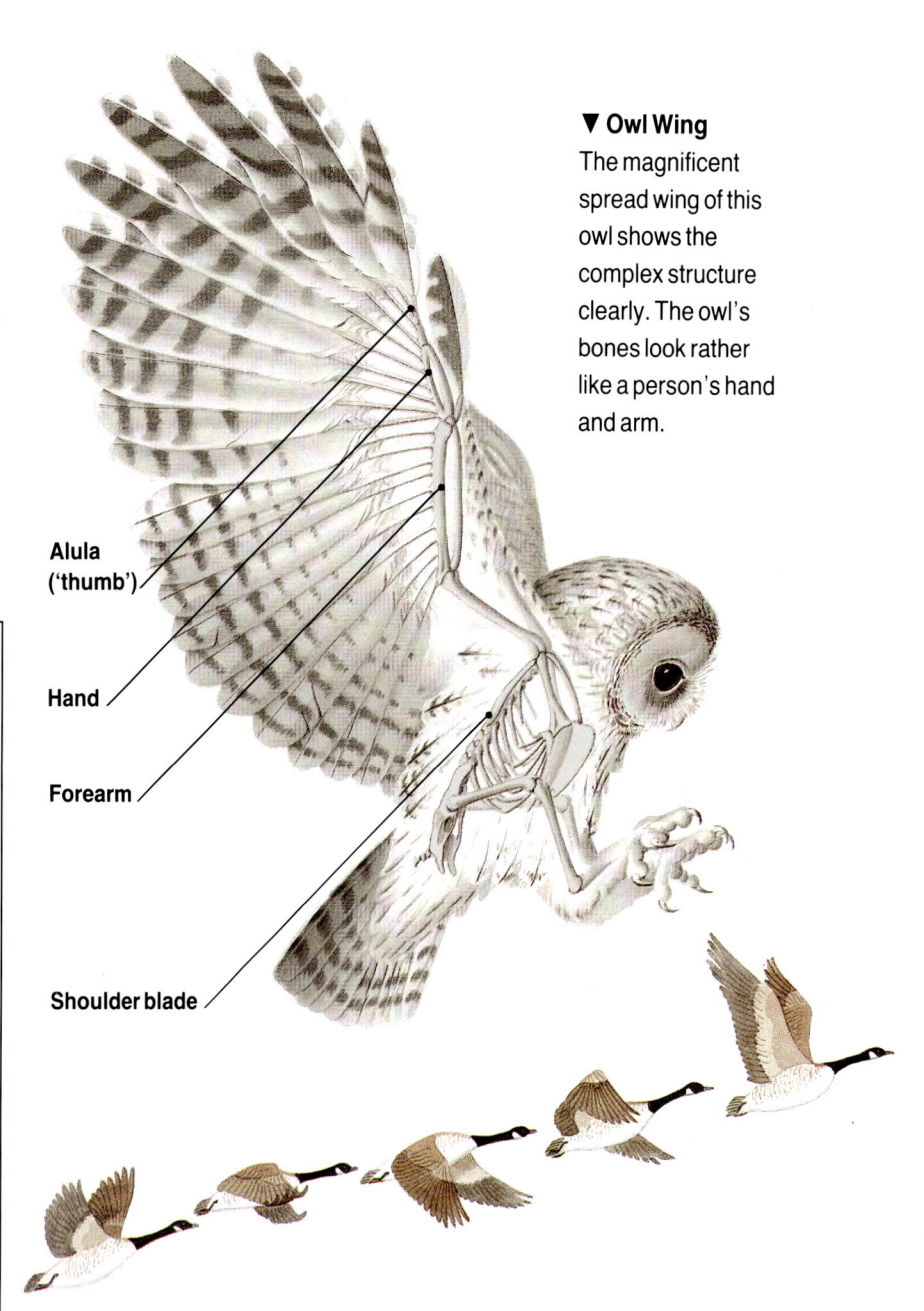

FEATHER FACTS

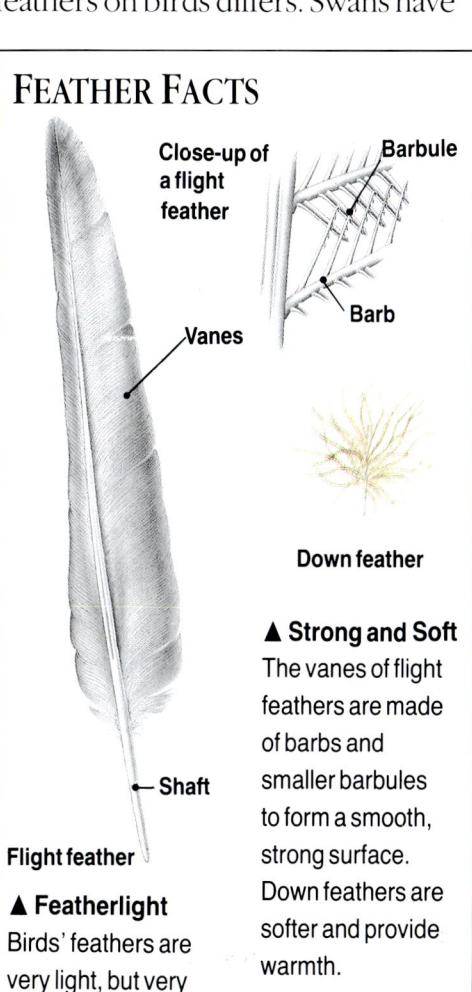

Close-up of a flight feather
Barbule
Vanes
Barb

Down feather

Shaft
Flight feather

▲ **Strong and Soft**
The vanes of flight feathers are made of barbs and smaller barbules to form a smooth, strong surface. Down feathers are softer and provide warmth.

▲ **Featherlight**
Birds' feathers are very light, but very strong. It is these feathers, together with powerful muscles and light bones, that make it possible for a bird to fly.

▼ **Owl Wing**
The magnificent spread wing of this owl shows the complex structure clearly. The owl's bones look rather like a person's hand and arm.

Alula ('thumb')
Hand
Forearm
Shoulder blade

▼ **Pheasant Chick**
The down feathers on this young pheasant chick are very easy to see.

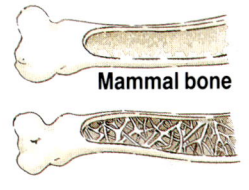

Mammal bone
Bird bone

▲ **Hollow Bones**
The bones of mammals are almost solid, but most bird bones are hollow, with struts inside to make them strong.

▲ **Flying Along**
By moving its wings up and down, a bird is able to take off and push itself forwards. Air pressure under the wings keeps the bird in the air. The outer part of the wings provides thrust. The mesh structure of the feathers stops them bending.

BIRDS AND BIRDWATCHING

KNOW YOUR BEAKS

The beak of a bird is a useful clue to its identity. But it can usually tell you something about what a bird eats and how it gets its food, too. Waders that dig deep into mud to find shellfish and tiny water creatures often have long, sometimes curving beaks. Birds such as finches that eat seeds and nuts usually have short, sturdy beaks to crack them with. Birds of prey have hooked beaks for tearing meat.

Kestrel

Mallard

Swift

Spotted flycatcher

Greenfinch

Cormorant

Oystercatcher

▶ **Feathery Pheasant**
A male pheasant has bright, colourful feathers. His tail feathers are very long and help to attract a mate. His beak is stout and sharp for picking berries, shoots, and grain.

the most – more than 25,000! Small birds, such as blue tits, have only about 1,500.

A bird is able to fly because of the shape of its wings, as well as its feather structure. Air passes over the top of the wings faster than it does the bottom, creating pressure under the wings. This is what lifts the bird. By flapping its wings downwards and backwards against the air, the bird flies forwards and gains height.

TAILS AND BEAKS

Birds' tails also differ in size and shape, so can act as identification clues. Some tails are functional, as on the treecreeper, where they provide support against a tree trunk. Others, such as a pheasant's colourful tail, can be purely decorative.

Birds do not have teeth. Instead the upper and lower jaws are elongated with a hard, nail-like covering to form a beak. (This is also sometimes called a bill.) A bird's beak is designed to help it collect food, as well as eat it, so varies greatly according to the lifestyle of the bird. For example, it may be hooked for tearing meat.

TAIL STORIES

Like beaks, tails can help you to identify a bird or to distinguish between two similar species. Get to know the main types, then match them to those you see on birdwatching trips.

Wedge-Shaped

Round

Square

Notched

Forked

CHANGING FEET

Birds' feet also differ depending on the bird's lifestyle. Many water birds, like ducks, have webs between their toes. As they swim, they simply bring their toes together and then spread them apart under water, which helps to push them forward.

Most birds have four toes, three pointing forwards and one backwards. Toes may differ in length, and claw length also varies. These variations help different birds to feed, walk, swim, grip, and balance on a branch or other perch.

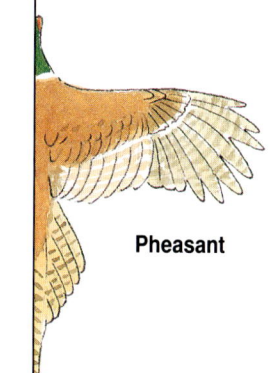

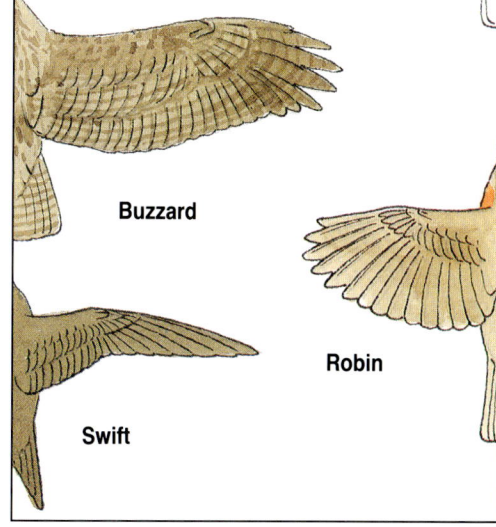

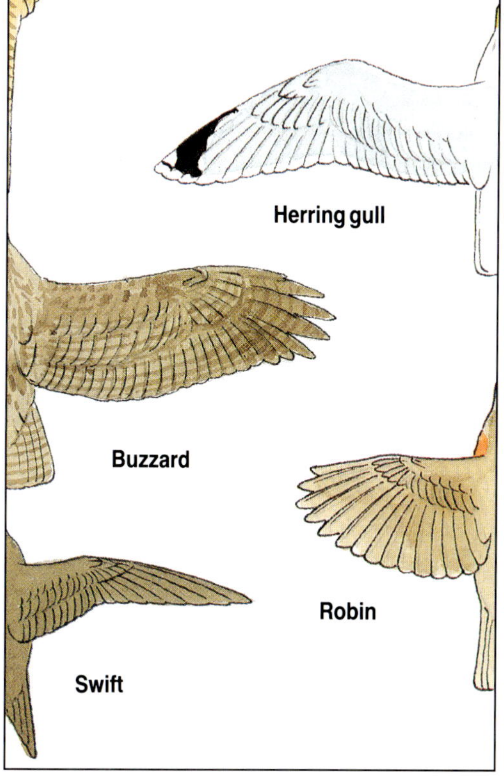

FEET FEATURES

Like their beaks, birds' feet give a clear sign of the way they live. Ducks, geese, swans, and gulls have webs between their toes to help them swim. Coots have long toes with flaps of skin for swimming and walking over mud. Birds of prey, such as eagles, have strong toes and sharp claws, called talons, for gripping their prey. Woodpeckers have two toes pointing forwards and two backwards to enable them to climb trees. Swifts, which rarely land, have four forward-pointing toes which allow them to cling on to a wall or rock face.

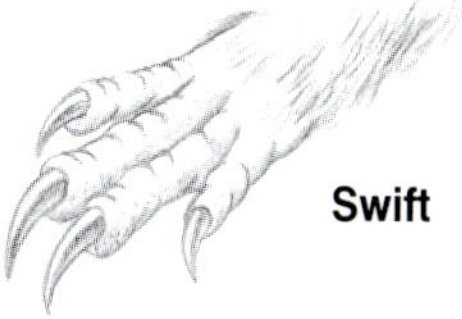

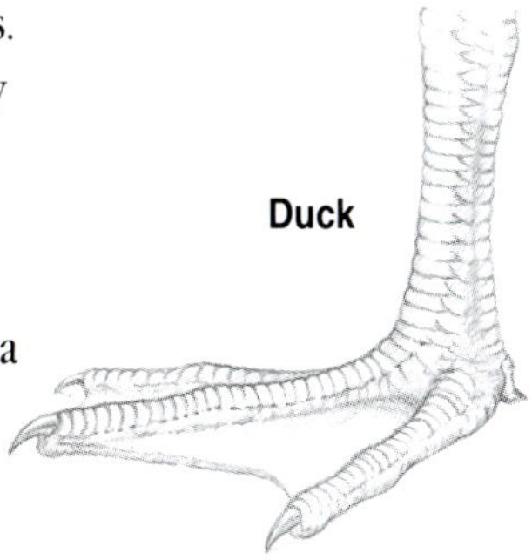

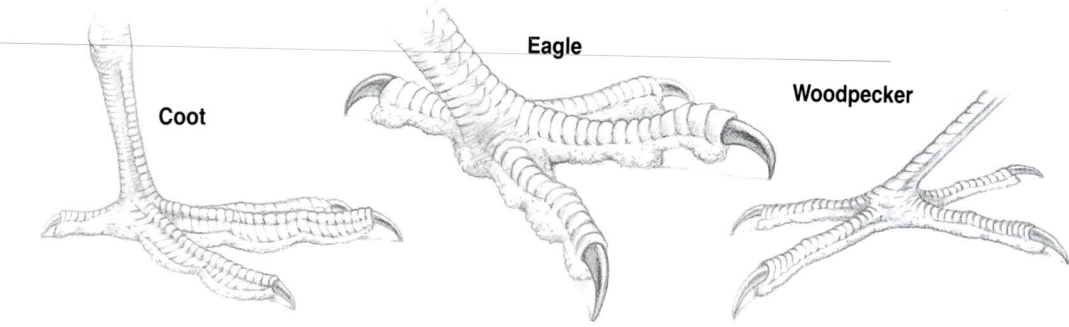

▲ **Built for Speed**
The kestrel has pointed wings and a long tail which enable it to hover and fly fast after its prey.

◀ **Swimming Flaps**
The flaps of skin which make it a powerful swimmer can be clearly seen on this coot's feet.

ON THE WING

The length and shape of its wings determine how a bird flies. Birds of prey, such as buzzards, have long, broad wings that enable them to soar across the skies. The narrow, pointed wings of birds like swifts make them agile and able to fly and turn rapidly.

Bird Behaviour

Becoming aware of how different birds behave will help you to identify them. Bird songs, their courtship habits, and how they establish territories are all helpful clues.

A bird song can be delightful for humans to listen to, but its real purposes are to attract a mate or announce a claim to a territory. Each species is able to recognize its own song and ignore the songs of other species. Many birds have very complicated and musical songs, while others, like the cuckoo, have a simple phrase of just a couple of notes that is repeated over and over.

It is generally only male birds that sing, although both males and females have call notes. These are the individual notes each bird makes, and some birds have up to 15. The notes are often repeated but they are not put together to make a song. A bird will use these call notes for many reasons – to beg for food, sound an alarm, contact another bird.

LOOK AT ME!

Male birds that do not have elaborate songs have other ways to attract a female. These are known as courtship displays and can involve exhibiting feathers and lots of movement, or a combination of both with song, depending on the species. Great crested grebes, for example, carry pieces of weed in their beaks and stretch their necks up, while goldcrests raise their crown feathers to display the colour underneath.

KEEP OUT!

The purpose of finding a mate is to breed, or produce young. To breed

DISPLAY FLIGHTS

Some birds, such as skylarks and sedge warblers, have special song flights as part of their courtship display, or to warn other birds off their territory.

▼ **Swan Dance**
This striking pair of mute swans is performing a ritual dance that takes place after mating. The sexes of this species look alike, but in fact one of the birds shown here is a male, the other one a female.

▲ **Singing Robin**
A robin proclaims his territory by singing loudly. He is warning off males while trying to impress a female.

BIRD BEHAVIOUR

◄ Skylarks slowly climb into the sky while singing their beautiful warbling song, before dropping rapidly back to the ground in a steep dive.

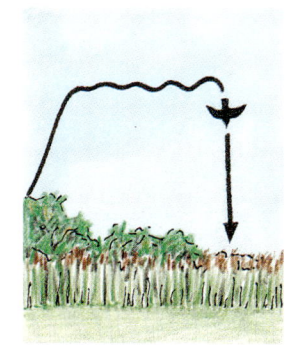

◄ Sedge warblers will sometimes fly up from grasses and continue in a rapid up-and-down motion until dropping back to the ground gently.

▼ **Fighting Fit**
It is rare for birds to fight and even the most violent-looking scraps only result in a few lost feathers. Coots use their beaks to peck at each other and sometimes throw themselves backwards to strike out with their feet. This is only a trial of strength and the loser will simply move off to find a quieter place.

successfully, a bird must find enough food and a suitable place to build its nest. Then it must keep out intruders. To do this the bird marks out its territory, that is the home it shares with a female during the breeding season. The territory has well-defined boundaries, which the male bird patrols. He selects regular 'song perches' along the edges of the territory where he sings to warn off other birds.

Some birds, like the short-eared owl, have large territories. These can be more than 1 square kilometre (⅘ square mile). Other birds such as the blackbird or robin, may live in a single garden.

◄ **Family Crest**
The goldcrest is one of Europe's smallest birds and a member of the kinglet family. Its coloured crown feathers are usually well hidden. However, during courtship or a fight with a rival, they may be raised and spread in a sudden and vivid splash of colour.

► **Kittiwake Colony**
Kittiwakes have small breeding territories. Thousands of pairs may breed together at one cliff face colony. Crowded onto cliff ledges, each bird defends just enough space for its nest and young and will only peck at a neighbouring bird if it strays too close.

21

BIRD LIFE CYCLES

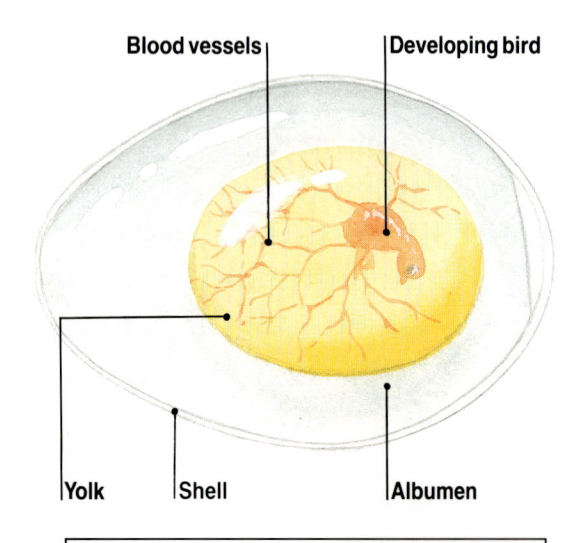

Blood vessels | Developing bird

Yolk | Shell | Albumen

◀ **Inside the Egg**
Birds' eggs are laid one at a time. They are made of a hard shell with the yolk and albumen (egg white) inside. The developing bird takes food from the yolk and oxygen through the shell. Birds which have feathered chicks lay large eggs.

CHICK TYPES

Some chicks are born naked, while others have feathers. Naked chicks must be kept warm and fed until their feathers grow. Chicks born with feathers are quite independent from the start.

▼ Lapwing chicks are born with brown feathers. These hide them from predators.

▲ Blackbird chicks are born naked. They grow feathers in about two weeks.

▶ **Species Survival**
The smaller a bird is, the more eggs it is likely to lay. Most small birds are eaten or die when young, so adult females like the blue tit, who may only live one year, lay up to 12 eggs at a time. The larger and stronger puffin may live for 30 years, and so will only lay one egg in each year.

When birds come together to mate they find a suitable place to build a nest. A nest is where birds lay their eggs, so it is important to find a site where the eggs or young will not be attacked.

One or both birds choose the site and build the nest. You will soon notice that nest sites differ between species. Nests can be built on the ground, in burrows, on tree branches, or in holes. Birds that have adapted to town life even use ledges and holes in buildings.

NEST TYPES

Nests come in all shapes and sizes. Open, cup-shaped nests are built by species such as blackbirds that shelter their young and eggs by sitting on the nests. Other nests are dome-shaped, and some are found in a hole or in a tree.

Most ground-nesting birds, like the pheasant, simply scratch a hollow in the ground. Other birds make complicated structures from grass, twigs, moss, or spiders' webs.

You must never disturb birds when they are building nests as they can be frightened away. Leave old nests if you find them. They may be used the following year.

BIRD LIFE CYCLES

NEW LIFE
Unlike mammals, where the young develop inside the mother, birds lay eggs. This allows the young to develop inside a protective shell. After mating, each egg is laid individually by the female.

Eggs must be kept warm. The female sits on the eggs for warmth, and this is called incubation. The incubation period varies from about 11 days for the skylark to about 40 days for the puffin. The young birds hatch by breaking out of the egg using a sharp point on their beak called the egg tooth.

◀ **Robin's Nest**
This is usually hidden in a tree or shed and built of dry grass and leaves. The young, with their bright throats, called gapes, beg the parent to feed them.

▼ **Speckled Eggs**
A lapwing's nest is a simple layer of grass. Its eggs are dark and speckled to hide them from enemies.

▶ **Feathery Home**
A long-tailed tit's nest is an amazing construction of spider's webs, feathers, moss, and other materials. As many as 2,000 feathers can be used in a single nest.

Large pine trees are a favourite nesting place for goldcrests, coal tits, and siskins.

Large broad-leaved trees like oaks are used for nesting by chaffinches, robins, woodpigeons, blue tits, and great spotted woodpeckers.

At woodland edges, plants like nettles and brambles, and thick clumps of grass provide ideal nesting places for birds like willow warblers and chiffchaffs.

TREE CHOICE
Different trees provide nesting places for different birds. Nests can be built near the top of a tree or on the ground nearby. However some birds prefer shrubs and grasses for their nest sites.

Turtle doves, chiffchaffs, willow warblers, and bullfinches are some of the birds which will nest in smaller broad-leaved or coniferous trees.

MIGRATION

Some birds fly great distances in search of food, areas to breed, and places to sleep, making an annual journey from a wintering area to a breeding area and back. This long-distance flight, crossing oceans and continents, is known as migration.

Some birds are born with an instinct that naturally tells them when it is time to migrate. They prepare for the journey by building up fat reserves, which provide all the energy they need during the flight.

Young birds migrating for the first time are often flying on their own to a winter home they have never seen before. They are able to sense their direction by using the sun, the moon, and the stars for guidance. Their natural instinct also ensures that they return to their place of birth the following year.

SEASONAL VISITORS
Birds that only live in northern Europe during the summer are

V FORMATION
Some birds, such as geese, migrate in flocks. They often travel in a V formation. This probably helps them by allowing each bird to fly in the slipstream (air pushed backwards by the wings) of the bird in front. Gulls often fly like this on the way to their roosts.

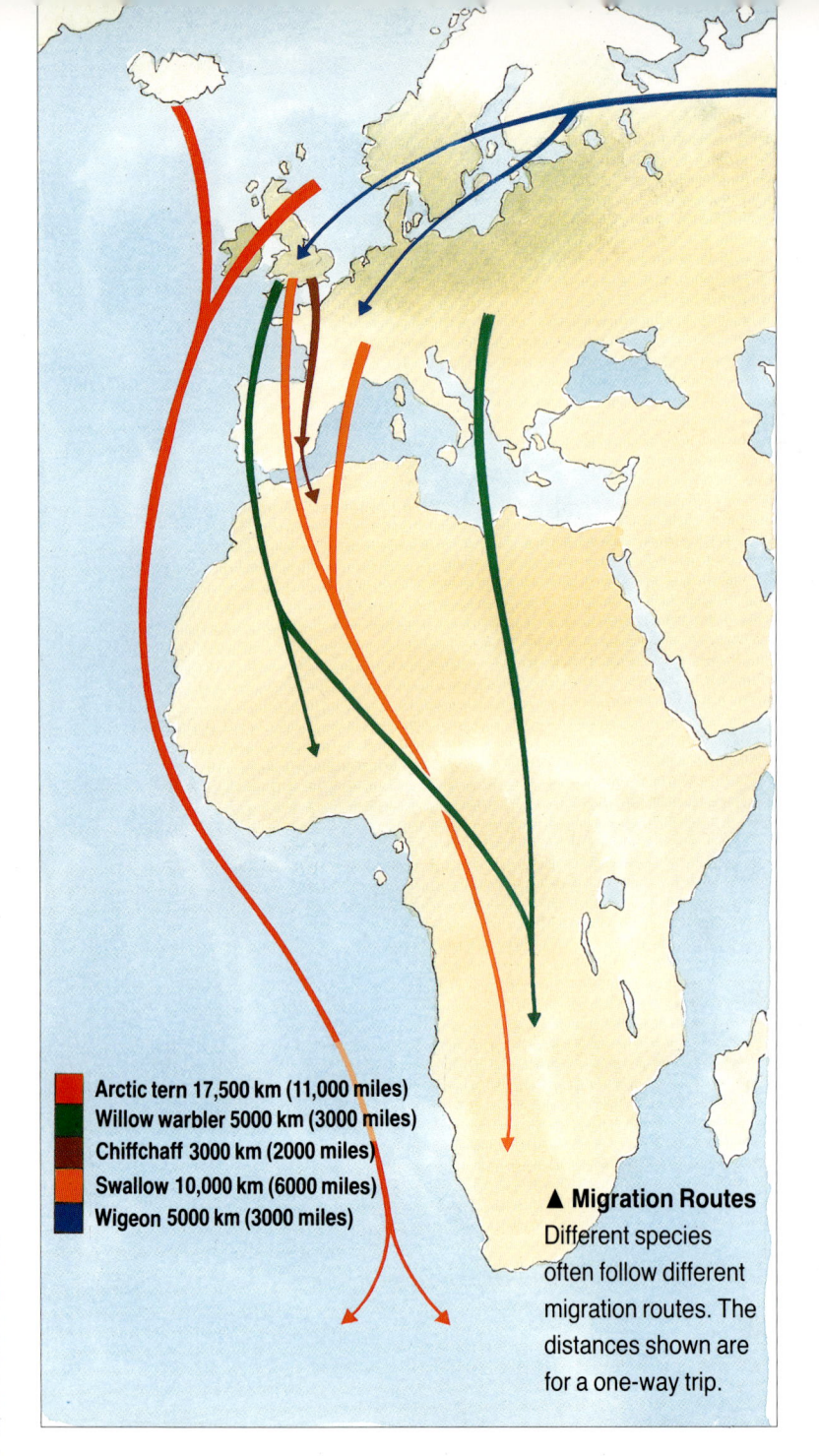

- Arctic tern 17,500 km (11,000 miles)
- Willow warbler 5000 km (3000 miles)
- Chiffchaff 3000 km (2000 miles)
- Swallow 10,000 km (6000 miles)
- Wigeon 5000 km (3000 miles)

▲ **Migration Routes**
Different species often follow different migration routes. The distances shown are for a one-way trip.

▶ **On the Wire**
House martins and swallows frequently collect in large flocks before migrating south in the autumn. These flocks are often made up of young birds who stay together during their journey to Africa.

called summer visitors. The most common summer visitors to Europe are willow warblers. Each autumn an estimated 900 million of them migrate south to Africa. Sadly, many of them do not survive the long journey. Some get too tired or meet bad weather, while others may be shot or trapped.

Some birds which breed in the far north – Greenland, Scandinavia, or Siberia – migrate south to spend the winter in Britain and northern Europe because it is warmer. These winter visitors include redwings and fieldfares, and many species of waders such as redshanks, dunlins, and sanderlings.

PASSING THROUGH

Some birds however, simply pass through Britain and northern Europe on their way south in the autumn, or going back north in the spring. Thousands stop and feed to replenish their energy stores before moving on. These birds are called passage migrants and are seen only in the spring and autumn.

▲ **Record Flight**
The Arctic tern migrates the furthest of any bird, an annual journey of 35,000 km (22,000 miles).

▼ **Night Traveller**
The redwing migrates at night and its thin 'seep' call note can often be heard on a dark winter's evening.

MIGRATION FACTS

● An estimated 5,000 million birds migrate from Europe to Africa every autumn. 900 million are willow warblers.

● Many birds double their weight before migrating to provide themselves with an energy store for the long flight.

● Some migrating birds travel 3000 kilometres (1800 miles) without stopping.

● Most migrating birds fly at heights of less than 1500 metres (5000 feet), but some can go as high as 6000 metres (20,000 feet).

BIRD PROFILES

The following pages describe the common habitats of Britain and northern Europe and the birds you are most likely to find there. Each chapter concentrates on one habitat, such as woodlands or coasts, and is followed by a special bird profile section. In these sections there is a close-up illustration of each bird, as well as all the detailed information you will need to make a positive identification.

Using the profiles, you will be able to identify 84 of the most frequently seen birds, and discover fascinating details about them. You can take the book out birdwatching with you and use the whole section as a field guide, or you can refer to it at home to identify a bird from your notes.

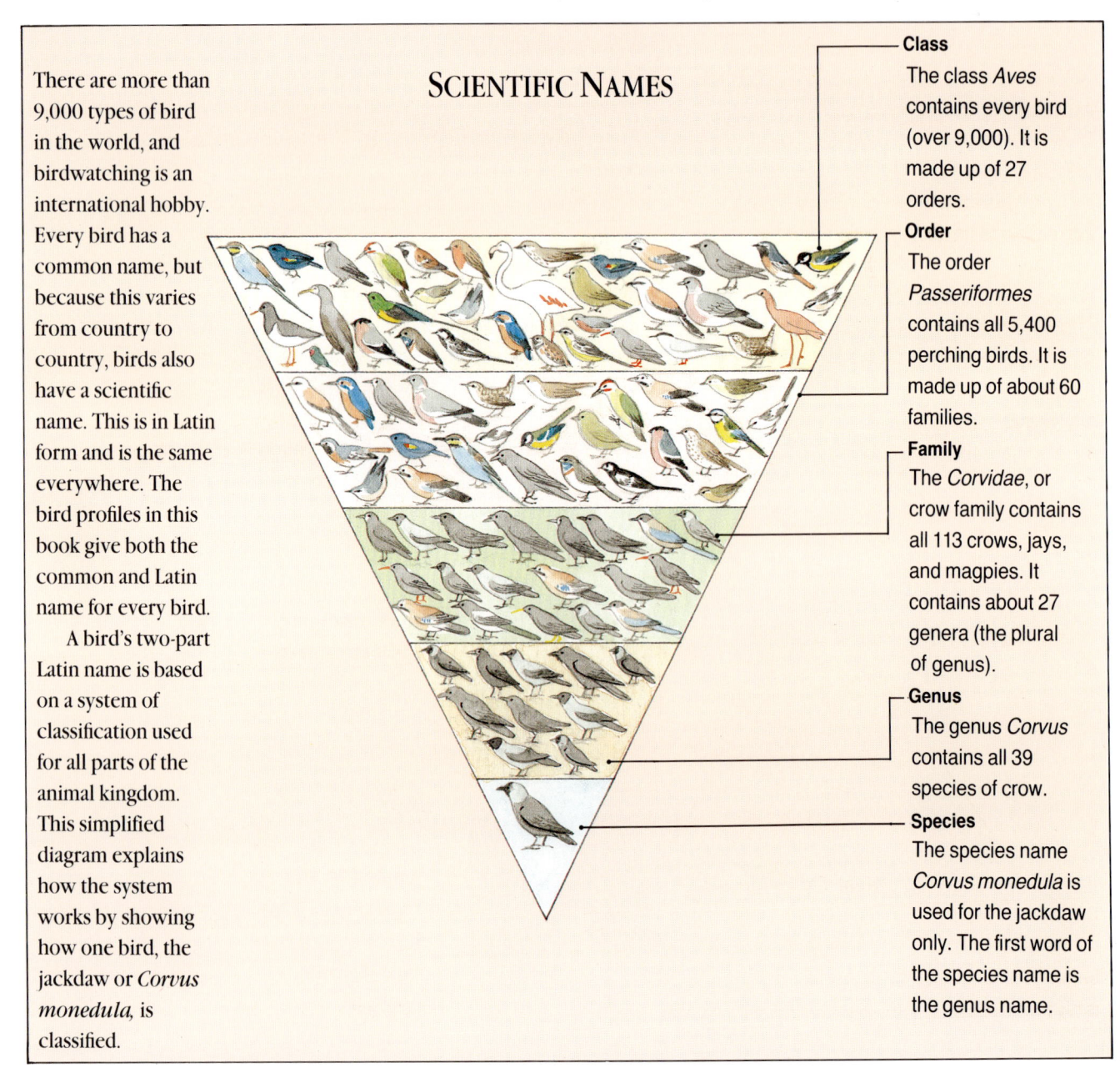

SCIENTIFIC NAMES

There are more than 9,000 types of bird in the world, and birdwatching is an international hobby. Every bird has a common name, but because this varies from country to country, birds also have a scientific name. This is in Latin form and is the same everywhere. The bird profiles in this book give both the common and Latin name for every bird.

A bird's two-part Latin name is based on a system of classification used for all parts of the animal kingdom. This simplified diagram explains how the system works by showing how one bird, the jackdaw or *Corvus monedula*, is classified.

Class
The class *Aves* contains every bird (over 9,000). It is made up of 27 orders.

Order
The order *Passeriformes* contains all 5,400 perching birds. It is made up of about 60 families.

Family
The *Corvidae*, or crow family contains all 113 crows, jays, and magpies. It contains about 27 genera (the plural of genus).

Genus
The genus *Corvus* contains all 39 species of crow.

Species
The species name *Corvus monedula* is used for the jackdaw only. The first word of the species name is the genus name.

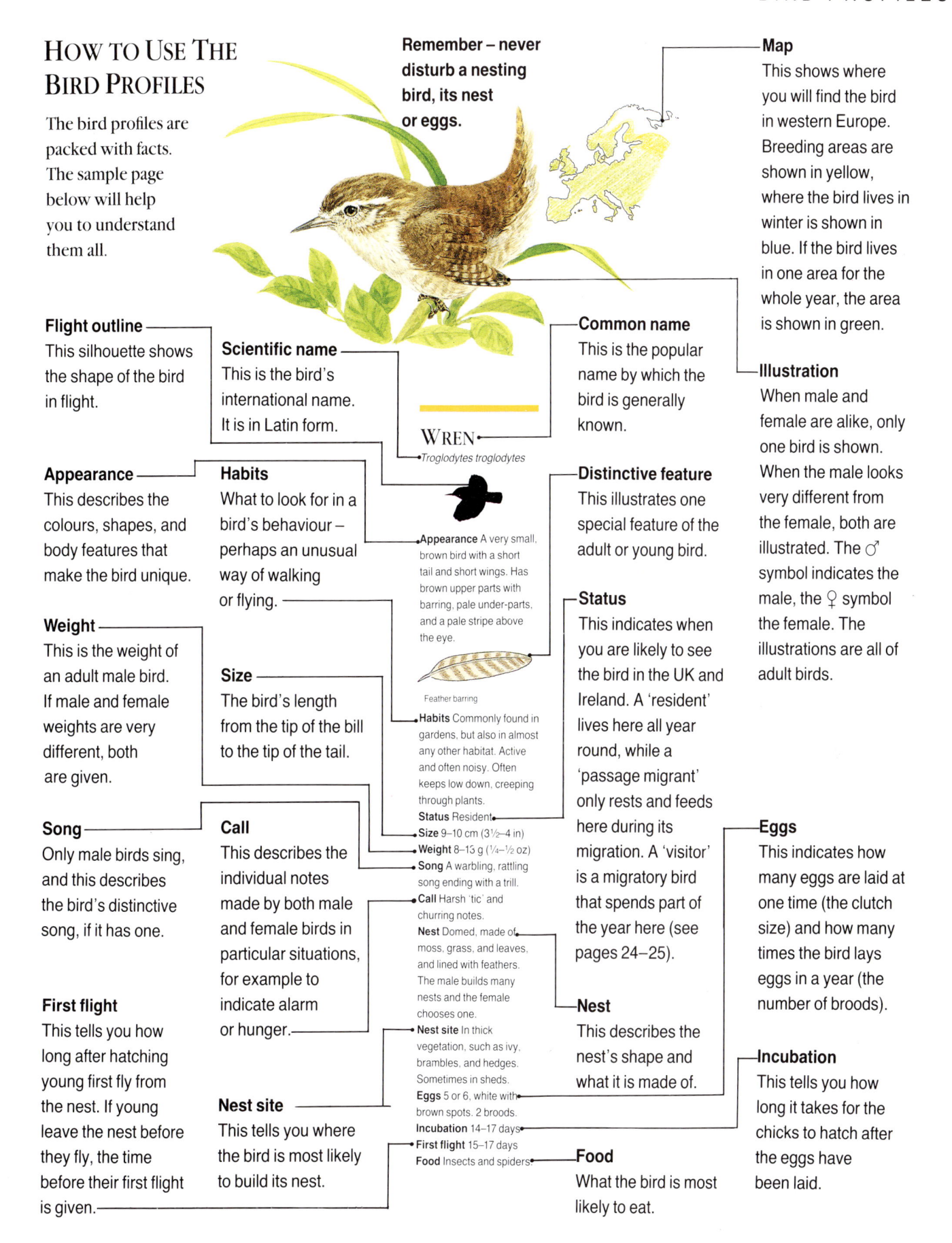

BIRD PROFILES

How to Use The Bird Profiles

The bird profiles are packed with facts. The sample page below will help you to understand them all.

Remember – never disturb a nesting bird, its nest or eggs.

Map
This shows where you will find the bird in western Europe. Breeding areas are shown in yellow, where the bird lives in winter is shown in blue. If the bird lives in one area for the whole year, the area is shown in green.

Flight outline
This silhouette shows the shape of the bird in flight.

Scientific name
This is the bird's international name. It is in Latin form.

Common name
This is the popular name by which the bird is generally known.

WREN
Troglodytes troglodytes

Illustration
When male and female are alike, only one bird is shown. When the male looks very different from the female, both are illustrated. The ♂ symbol indicates the male, the ♀ symbol the female. The illustrations are all of adult birds.

Appearance
This describes the colours, shapes, and body features that make the bird unique.

Habits
What to look for in a bird's behaviour – perhaps an unusual way of walking or flying.

Appearance A very small, brown bird with a short tail and short wings. Has brown upper parts with barring, pale under-parts, and a pale stripe above the eye.

Distinctive feature
This illustrates one special feature of the adult or young bird.

Feather barring

Status
This indicates when you are likely to see the bird in the UK and Ireland. A 'resident' lives here all year round, while a 'passage migrant' only rests and feeds here during its migration. A 'visitor' is a migratory bird that spends part of the year here (see pages 24–25).

Weight
This is the weight of an adult male bird. If male and female weights are very different, both are given.

Size
The bird's length from the tip of the bill to the tip of the tail.

Habits Commonly found in gardens, but also in almost any other habitat. Active and often noisy. Often keeps low down, creeping through plants.
Status Resident
Size 9–10 cm (3½–4 in)
Weight 8–13 g (¼–½ oz)
Song A warbling, rattling song ending with a trill.
Call Harsh 'tic' and churring notes.
Nest Domed, made of moss, grass, and leaves, and lined with feathers. The male builds many nests and the female chooses one.
Nest site In thick vegetation, such as ivy, brambles, and hedges. Sometimes in sheds.
Eggs 5 or 6, white with brown spots. 2 broods.
Incubation 14–17 days
First flight 15–17 days
Food Insects and spiders

Song
Only male birds sing, and this describes the bird's distinctive song, if it has one.

Call
This describes the individual notes made by both male and female birds in particular situations, for example to indicate alarm or hunger.

Nest
This describes the nest's shape and what it is made of.

Eggs
This indicates how many eggs are laid at one time (the clutch size) and how many times the bird lays eggs in a year (the number of broods).

First flight
This tells you how long after hatching young first fly from the nest. If young leave the nest before they fly, the time before their first flight is given.

Nest site
This tells you where the bird is most likely to build its nest.

Food
What the bird is most likely to eat.

Incubation
This tells you how long it takes for the chicks to hatch after the eggs have been laid.

27

Town and Garden Birds

Many woodland birds whose natural habitat has been destroyed now live in towns and gardens. These are natural places for you to start birdwatching. You can see different birds just walking to and from school, your friends' homes, or the shops. Your own front and back gardens will have some birds for you to observe and identify, too.

Natural food may be scarce in gardens. This is because some trees are ornamental and do not provide a home for enough insects that birds can feed on. If you or your parents plant trees such as willow or silver birch, you should attract a variety of birds. Another way to bring birds into your garden is to provide them with food and water. A bird table or a bird bath will bring in visitors to drink or

▲ **Thirsty Birds**
A variety of ducks have gathered around this suburban pond in search of drinking water. Most natural water sources are good places for birdwatching. If you put a bird bath in your garden at home, it will also attract many birds for you to look at.

TOWN AND GARDEN BIRDS

bathe. In harsh winters when snow covers the ground, watch out for more unusual birds, such as fieldfares (see page 64), that may visit gardens in search of food.

One of the best places for birdwatching near your home is probably a park. Look for one with a range of trees and plenty of bushes and shrubs. This is where you will see the biggest variety of birds. A lake or a pond also always attracts birds. This is because clean water for drinking and bathing is often difficult to find in built-up areas.

▲ **Food Fun**
Food scraps and seeds are ideal for a bird tray. Here, the boy is tying on dry seed heads, while the other children are adding suet pieces covered with seeds. They have also hung peanuts on a string. You can make feeders from many everyday items (see page 30).

STOCKING A BIRD TABLE

Keeping a bird tray or feeder well stocked with a supply of food is a good way to attract a variety of birds.

Just like humans, different birds prefer different foods. Here is a list of foods you can put out and the birds each is likely to attract.

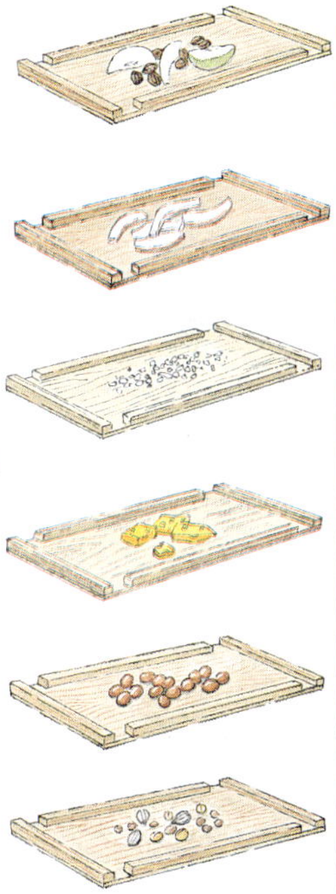

- **Apples and sultanas**
Blackbirds, fieldfares, redwings, and thrushes
- **Bacon rind (chopped)**
Robins, tits
- **Breadcrumbs**
Starlings, robins, and thrushes
- **Cheese**
Robins, tits
- **Peanuts**
Greenfinches, nuthatches, and tits
- **Wild bird seed mixtures**
Many birds

MAKING FEEDERS

It need not cost much to make feeders that you can tie in trees or on bird tables. All you need are left over food containers, a small log from the garden, and some nuts, seeds, and suet.

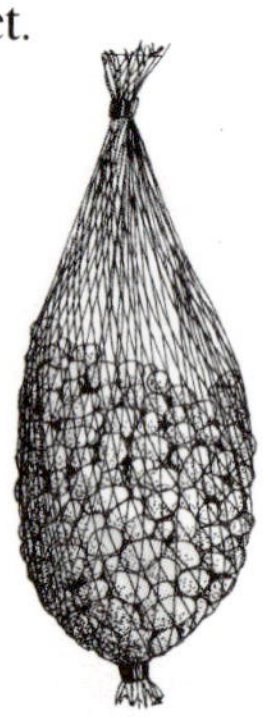

▲ Try filling the fine mesh bags that oranges or onions are sold in with nuts and food scraps.

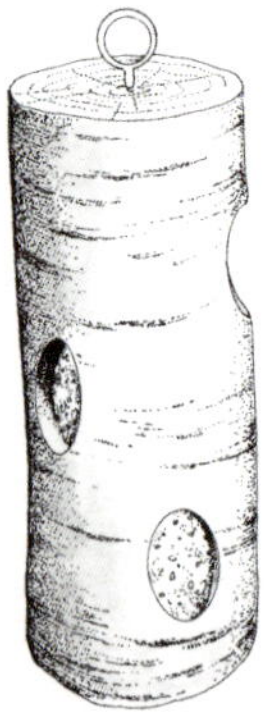

▲ Ask an adult to drill holes in a small log. Do *not* attempt to do this yourself. Fill the holes with suet to attract blue tits, then put a hook in the top to hang it up.

▲ Seed Snack
A plastic cup can make a good container for bird seed. Mix seeds together with lard.

CITY LIFE

All the buildings and lights in town and city centres mean that they are slightly warmer than the surrounding countryside. Some birds deliberately roost in towns for this reason. This is why you can often see starlings lined up along building ledges or gathering in trees at dusk.

▼ Tasty Crumbs
Some birds prefer to eat on the ground. Scatter left-over bread or cake in your garden to tempt them.

▼ Bird in the Hand
This male chaffinch, with his attractive colouring, tamely feasts on seeds.

NEST BOXES

Putting a nest box in your garden means you will be able to watch a bird building its nest and feeding its young. Be careful to position your nest box out of the wind and tilted down away from the rain.

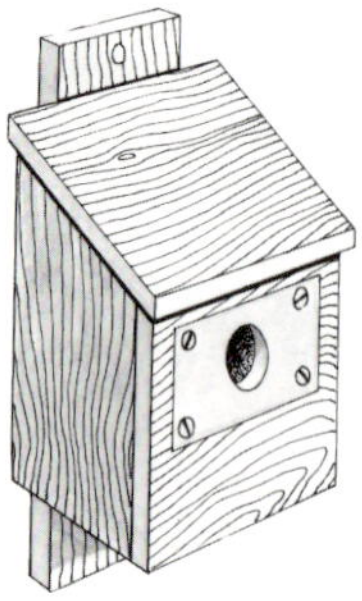

▲ Nest boxes with a small round hole are popular with tits.

▲ Flycatchers like to nest in open-fronted boxes.

Swifts and house martins have adapted to town life so well that most now breed on buildings. Swifts use small holes leading to spaces under the roof of a house to build their nests. They have to nest up high because they cannot take off from the ground. Some wild birds from the open countryside, such as kestrels (see page 58), have also adapted to life in towns. They nest on buildings and feed on mice and small birds. Sparrowhawks (see page 44) have also learned that bird tables in gardens attract small birds that they can feed on.

Town birds are often much tamer than their country cousins. Woodpigeons, shy in the country, feed alongside domestic pigeons in town. This is probably because they do not have to fear hunters' guns.

But life is not without danger for town birds. Cats are a constant threat. Often small garden bushes and trees do not provide adequate protection. Also, magpies, crows, and jays, as well as squirrels, raid nests and eat the eggs or nestlings. Cars are also a hazard for birds in towns. They hit and kill many birds, especially unwary youngsters.

▲ **Bumper Home**
Swallows often nest in a barn, but this one has chosen a lorry bumper. The eggs are incubated for 14–16 days. The chicks will leave after about 17 days.

PLANT FOOD FOR BIRDS

A well-stocked garden, full of flowering plants and trees, will attract a wide variety of birds for you to watch. Birds like plants because some, such as holly, produce berries they can eat, while others, like sunflowers, produce edible seeds. Many plants are home to all sorts of insects, too, which are another good food source. Gardens are also popular because bushes and branches provide birds with places to roost and build nests.

◀ Thistles are a good food source for goldfinches and linnets. A variety of birds eat nettles.

◀▼ Holly berries attract mistle thrushes, fieldfares, and redwings.

▶ Sunflower seeds attract finches and tits. Keep some seeds and put them out for birds in winter.

▶ Dandelion seeds are a favourite for many birds.

TOWN AND GARDEN BIRDS

COLLARED DOVE
Streptopelia decaocto

Appearance A pale brown-grey bird with a long tail and distinctive black half-collar on the back of its neck. The wings are darker brown than the body. Young birds have no collar.
Habits Found in towns, villages, and farms. Feeds on the ground and flies with a rapid and direct flight. Perches openly on roofs, branches, and wires.
Status Resident.
Size 32 cm (12¾ in)
Weight 150–225 g (5⅓–8 oz)
Song A deep 'coo-cooo-cu'.
Call A moaning 'kwurr', usually given in flight.
Nest A flimsy platform of twigs.
Nest site In trees, especially conifers, or on buildings.
Eggs 2, white. 2 or 3 broods.
Incubation 14–16 days
First flight 15–17 days
Food Grain and seeds.

Young head with no collar

Collared dove

Rock dove

ROCK DOVE (Feral Pigeon)
Columba livia

Appearance True wild birds are pale blue-grey with 2 black wing bars, a white rump, and a green and purple patch on the side of the neck. The domestic, or feral pigeon, comes in a variety of colours.
Habits The wild bird is confined to rocky coasts and inland cliffs. The very tame domestic variety is found in most towns.
Status Resident.
Size 33 cm (13 in)
Weight 240–300 g (8½–11 oz)
Call A cooing 'coo-roo-coo'.
Nest A few sticks and twigs.
Nest site On ledges and in holes in buildings.
Eggs 2, white. 3 or 4 broods.
Incubation 16–19 days
First flight 35–37 days
Food Grain, seeds, bread, and scraps.

Racing pigeon's ringed leg

TOWN AND GARDEN BIRDS

SWIFT
Apus apus

Appearance Sooty-black with long, narrow, pointed wings and a short, forked tail. Has a pale throat and short legs.

Small foot

Habits Found around towns and cities. All of its time away from the nest is spent flying. Flies rapidly with fast twists and turns. Often forms noisy, screaming groups.
Status Summer visitor.
Size 16 cm (6½ in)
Weight 36–50 g (1¼–1¾ oz)
Call Shrill, screaming 'sweeer'.

Large, gaping beak

Nest A small cup of tiny bits of straw and feathers glued together with saliva.
Nest site Mainly inside roof spaces.
Eggs 2 or 3, white. 1 brood.
Incubation 18–25 days
First flight 37–56 days
Food Insects caught in flight.

Swift

House martin

HOUSE MARTIN
Delichon urbica

Appearance Black and white with a short, forked tail. Has blue-black upper parts with a white rump and white under-parts.

Feathered foot

Habits Breeds around houses but often feeds near water. Spends most of its time in flight, often in the company of swallows (see page 62) but has a less swooping flight than a swallow.
Status Summer visitor.
Size 12 cm (4¾ in)
Weight 15–21 g (about ⅔ oz)
Song A squeaky twittering.
Call A quiet 'chirrrup'.
Nest Enclosed cup of mud with feathers and grass.
Nest site Against a wall, under eaves, and sometimes on cliffs.
Eggs 4 or 5, white. 2 or 3 broods.
Incubation 14–15 days
First flight 19–22 days
Food Insects caught in flight.

TOWN AND GARDEN BIRDS

WREN
Troglodytes troglodytes

Appearance A very small, brown bird with a short tail and short wings. Has brown upper parts with barring, pale under-parts, and a pale stripe above the eye.

Feather barring

Habits Commonly found in gardens, but also in almost any other habitat. Active and often noisy. Often keeps low down, creeping through plants.
Status Resident.
Size 9–10 cm (3½–4 in)
Weight 8–13 g (¼–½ oz)
Song A warbling, rattling song ending with a trill.
Call Harsh 'tic' and churring notes.
Nest Domed, made of moss, grass, and leaves, and lined with feathers. The male builds many nests and the female chooses one.
Nest site In thick vegetation, such as ivy, brambles, and hedges. Sometimes in sheds.
Eggs 5 or 6, white with brown spots. 2 broods.
Incubation 14–17 days
First flight 15–17 days
Food Insects and spiders.

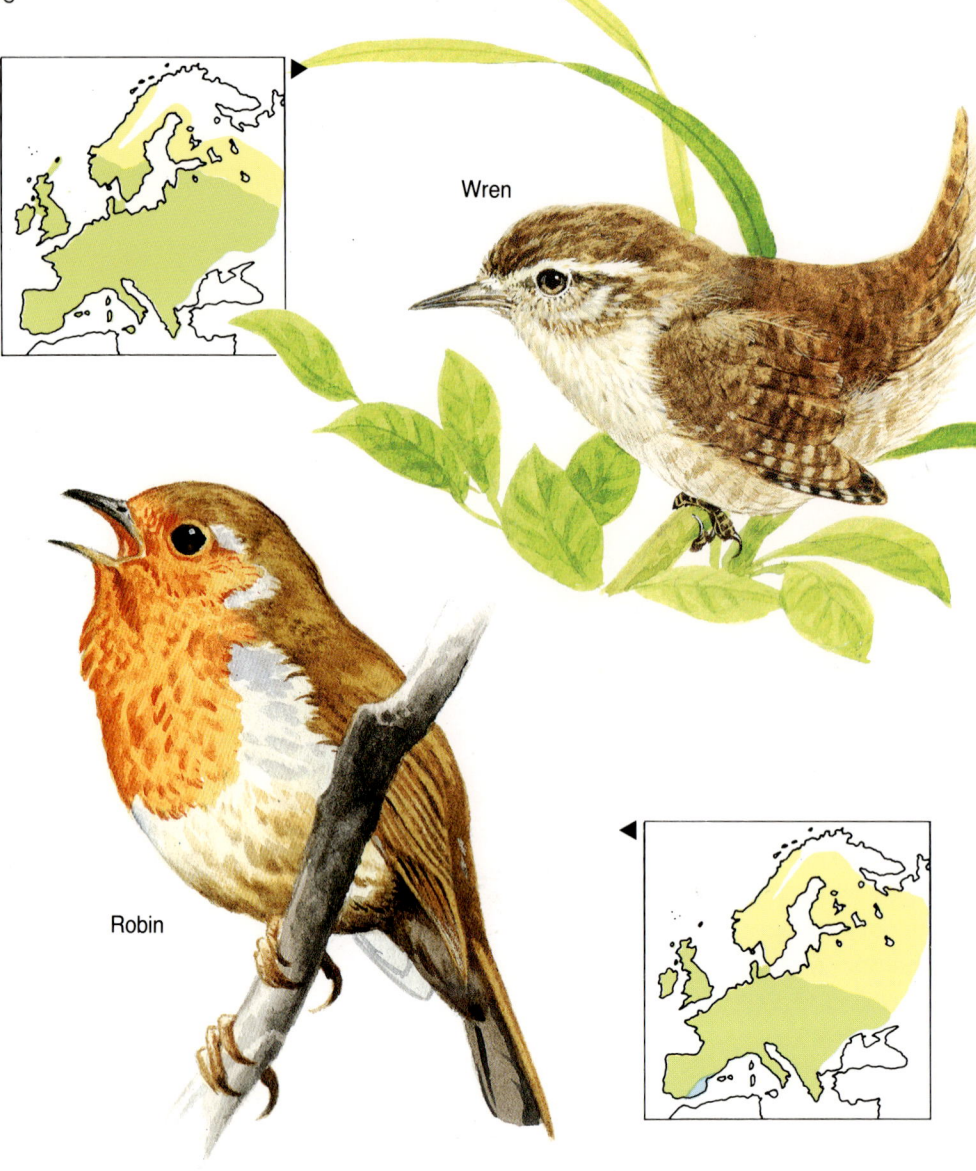

Wren

Robin

ROBIN
Erithacus rubecula

Appearance The orange breast of the adult is distinctive. Young robins are brown with buff spots.
Habits Quite tame and usually seen alone. Perches in low branches and hops on the ground.

Plumage on a young bird

Status Resident.
Size 14 cm (5½ in)
Weight 16–22 g (½–¾ oz)
Song A clear, high warbling, that is sadder and thinner in autumn.
Call A sharp 'tic' and thin 'tsee'.
Nest Domed, made of leaves, roots, and hairs.
Nest site In ivy or undergrowth, often near the base of a tree. Uses open-fronted nest boxes.
Eggs 4–6, white with small, red spots. 1 or 2 broods.
Incubation 13–14 days
First flight 12–15 days
Food Insects, worms, small seeds, and berries.

TOWN AND GARDEN BIRDS

BLACKBIRD
Turdus merula

Blackbird

Appearance The male is all black with an orange beak. The female is dark brown above with paler under-parts, sometimes slightly red-brown, and has a yellow-brown beak.
Habits Found in gardens and parks. Likes open grass. Raises tail on landing and runs or hops. Often perches on treetops and roofs to sing.
Status Resident.
Size 25 cm (10 in)
Weight 80–110 g (2¾–4 oz)
Song A fluty warbling with varied phrases.
Call A 'chook, chook' and a scolding 'chik-chik- chik'.
Nest An open cup of moss, grass, and mud lined with fine grass.
Nest site In bushes, trees, or sheds.

Singing blackbird

Eggs 3–5, green-blue with brown spots. 2 or 3 broods.
Incubation 13–15 days
First flight 13–15 days
Food Worms, insects, berries, and fruit.

SONG THRUSH
Turdus philomelos

Appearance Has brown upper parts and white under-parts with a buff breast. The breast and upper belly are covered with black spots. In flight the under-wings are yellow-buff.
Habits Found in gardens and parks. Stands fairly upright and feeds in the open. Smashes snails against stones with its beak to open their shells.

Smashing a snail shell

Status Resident. Summer and winter visitor in some parts of Europe.
Size 23 cm (9 in)
Weight 65–90 g (2⅓–3 oz)
Song Loud musical phrases repeated 2 or 3 times.
Call Soft 'tsipp' and loud 'tchuk'.
Nest Moss, grass, and leaves lined with mud.
Nest site In bushes, trees, and ivy.
Eggs 3–5, light blue with black spots. 2 broods.
Incubation 12–14 days
First flight 12–15 days
Food Worms, snails, insects, berries, and fruit.

Song thrush

35

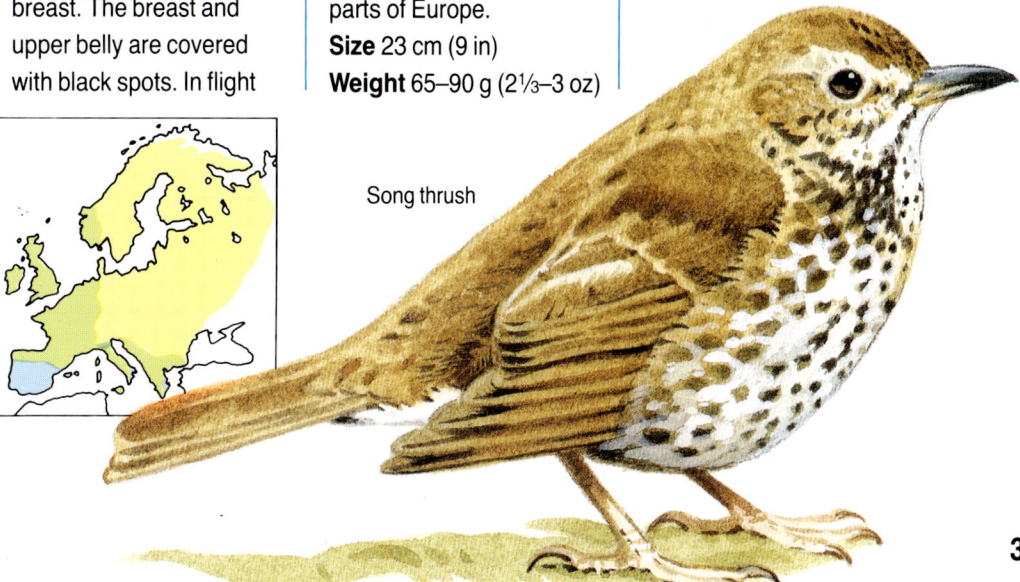

TOWN AND GARDEN BIRDS

BLUE TIT
Parus caeruleus

Appearance A small, blue, white, and yellow bird with a blue crown, wings, and tail, green back, and yellow under-parts. The white face and cheeks have a black line through each eye.

Hanging from a nut feeder

Habits Found in gardens and parks, often visiting bird tables. Hangs from tree branches in search of food. Forms flocks with other tits in winter.
Status Resident.
Size 11.5 cm (4½ in)
Weight 9–12 g (about ⅓ oz)
Song A series of high notes merging into a trill.
Call High 'tsee-tsee-tsit' and 'si-si-su-su-su'.
Nest A cup of moss and grass lined with feathers.
Nest site A hole in a tree or in nest boxes.
Eggs 6–12, white with red spots. 1 brood.
Incubation 13–14 days
First flight 18–20 days
Food Insects, seeds, and nuts. Peanuts at bird table.

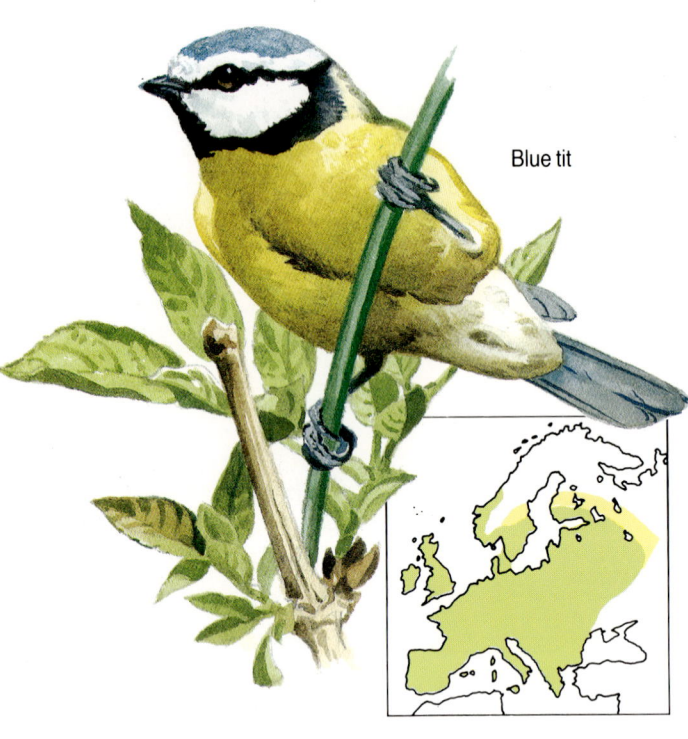

Blue tit

GREAT TIT
Parus major

Appearance The largest of the tits. Has a black head with white cheeks, green back, blue wings, and blue tail with white edges. The yellow under-parts have a broad black stripe down the centre of the belly. The female has a narrow black belly stripe.
Habits Found in gardens and parks, commonly at bird tables. Hangs acrobatically when searching for food. Often fights off smaller tits. Joins flocks of other tits in winter.
Status Resident.
Size 14 cm (5½ in)
Weight 16–21 g (⅔ oz)
Song A loud 'tee-chew, tee-chew, tee-chew'.
Call A high 'tsee' and a loud 'cha-cha-cha'.
Nest A cup of moss and grass lined with hair and wool.
Nest site A hole in a tree or a wall or in nest boxes.

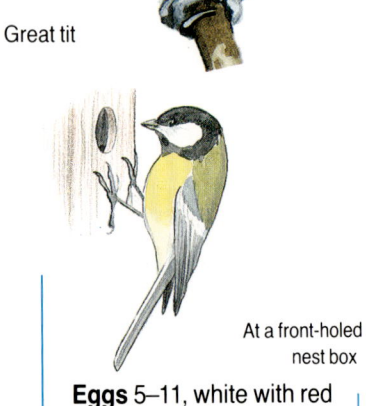

Great tit

At a front-holed nest box

Eggs 5–11, white with red spots. 1 brood.
Incubation 12–14 days
First flight 19–21 days
Food Insects, seeds, and nuts. Peanuts at bird table.

TOWN AND GARDEN BIRDS

JACKDAW
Corvus monedula

Appearance A crow with a small, black cap, a grey neck, and pale eyes. Its beak is fairly short.

Outstretched wings in flight

Habits Found in wooded gardens and parks, and around old buildings. Feeds mainly on the ground and is often found in flocks, sometimes with other crows.
Status Resident.
Size 33 cm (13 in)
Weight 220–270 g (7¾–10 oz)
Call A loud 'keeaw' or 'chack'.
Nest An open nest of sticks lined with wool.
Nest site A hole in a tree or building.
Eggs 4–6, pale blue with dark brown spots. 1 brood.
Incubation 18–19 days
First flight 30–35 days
Food Insects, worms, slugs, mice, and berries.

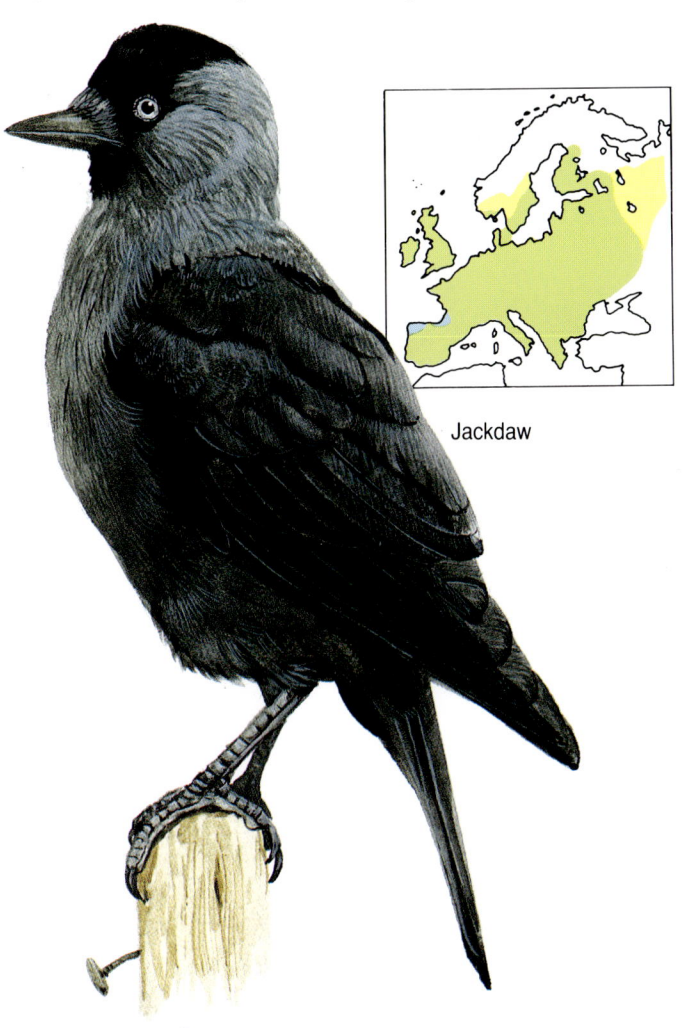

Jackdaw

Starling

STARLING
Sturnus vulgaris

Appearance Plump with a short tail and a long beak. Its black feathers have a green and purple gloss, and white spots in winter. The yellow beak has a blue base in males and a pink base in females.

Male's beak with blue base

Habits Found commonly in towns and gardens. Frequently seen in flocks, especially in winter. Runs quickly on the ground.
Status Resident and winter visitor.
Size 21 cm (8½ in)
Weight 75–90 g (2½–3 oz)
Song A high, varied warbling, whistling, and chirruping.
Call A harsh 'tcheer'.
Nest An untidy cup of grass with feathers.
Nest site A hole in a tree or building. Will use hole-fronted nest boxes.
Eggs 4–6, pale blue. 1 or 2 broods.
Incubation 12–13 days
First flight 20–22 days
Food Insects, worms, fruit, seeds, and berries. Readily feeds from bird tables.

TOWN AND GARDEN BIRDS

DUNNOCK
Prunella modularis

Appearance Sparrow-like with brown upper parts, grey head and under-parts, and a fine beak.
Habits Found in gardens and parks. Slightly timid. It hops and shuffles along the ground, often flicking its wings.
Status Resident.
Size 14 cm (5½ in)
Weight 19–24 g (about ¾ oz)
Song A musical, high warbling.
Call A clear 'tseep' and a high trill.
Nest A cup of twigs, moss, and leaves lined with hair or wool.
Nest site In bushes or hedges, sometimes in ivy.
Eggs 4 or 5, blue. 2 broods.
Incubation 12–13 days
First flight 12 days
Food Insects and small seeds.

Insect-eating beak

HOUSE SPARROW
Passer domesticus

Appearance The male has a brown back and neck with a grey crown and rump, a black throat, and a short white wing bar. In winter only the chin is black. The female has brown upper parts with a pale stripe over each eye. Both have pale under-parts.
Habits Found commonly in towns and gardens. Forms flocks and can be very tame. Feeds on the ground.
Status Resident.

Male's winter throat patch

Size 14.5 cm (5¾ in)
Weight 22–32 g (about 1 oz)
Song A series of chirruping notes.
Call A loud 'chee-ip' and a rapid twittering.
Nest An untidy dome of grass lined with feathers.
Nest site A hole in a building, or in bushes or ivy.
Eggs 3–6, white with dark spots. 2 or 3 broods.
Incubation 12–14 days
First flight 14–16 days
Food Seeds and insects.

House sparrow

♀
♂

Dunnock

TOWN AND GARDEN BIRDS

GREENFINCH
Carduelis chloris

Appearance A plump bird with a stout beak and a short, forked tail. The male has greenish upper parts, yellow-green under-parts, and a yellow strip down the wing, with yellow in the tail. The female is much browner with faint streaks on upper parts.

Male in flight

Habits Common in gardens and parks. Feeds on the ground and forms flocks in winter. Has a butterfly-like display flight in spring.
Status Resident.
Size 14.5 cm (5¾ in)
Weight 25–34 g (about 1 oz)
Song Twittering phrases with a long 'tsweee'.
Call A trill in flight and 'chup' or 'tsooee'.
Nest A cup of twigs and moss lined with fine grass.
Nest site In shrubs, bushes, or low trees.
Eggs 4–6, whitish with dark marks. 2 broods.
Incubation 13–14 days
First flight 13–16 days
Food Seeds and insects. Eats peanuts and sunflower seeds at a bird table.

Greenfinch

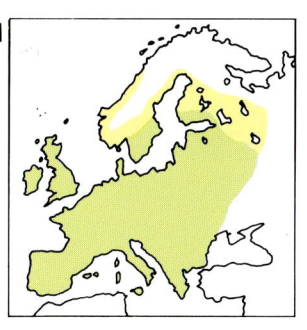

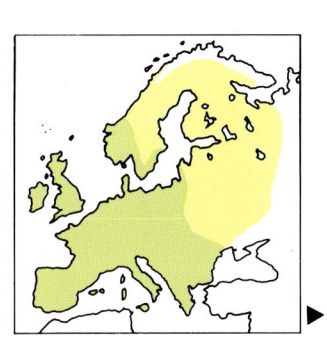

Chaffinch

CHAFFINCH
Fringilla coelebs

Appearance The male has a blue-grey head, red-brown back, green rump and pink-brown cheeks and under-parts. The tail is slightly forked with white edges and each wing has 2 white wing bars. The female is brown above with brown-grey under-parts.

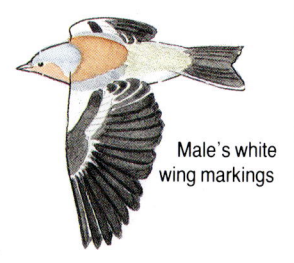

Male's white wing markings

Habits Found in gardens and parks. Feeds on the ground and forms flocks in winter. Has a rather bouncing flight.
Status Resident and winter visitor.
Size 15 cm (6 in)
Weight 19–24 g (about ¾ oz)
Song A loud series of notes with a flourish at the end.
Call A loud 'pink, pink' and a 'tupe' in flight.
Nest A neat cup of grass, moss, and lichens lined with hair.
Nest site In a bush or tree.
Eggs 4 or 5, pale blue with dark spots. 1 brood.
Incubation 12–13 days
First flight 13–14 days
Food Seeds and insects. Feeds from bird tables.

39

Woodland Birds

▼ Look and Listen
Adult birdwatchers compare notes and use a field guide to check which species they have seen. The children study remains of nuts and berries to help identify birds.

During the summer months, birdwatching in woodland can be frustrating because the leaf cover makes birds hard to see. Try waiting at the edge of a pond or lake to glimpse them as they come to drink, or simply watch and listen patiently.

In the winter, woodlands can seem empty of birds. But if you listen carefully for calls you may be able to find flocks made up of a variety of small birds, such as tits, goldcrests, and treecreepers. Flocks of finches and buntings (see pages 39 and 79) may be found feeding on the edges of a wood.

TREE TYPES
Trees can be roughly divided into deciduous or broad-leaved trees, which lose their leaves in winter, and

▶ Nut Cracker
The nuthatch is able to walk up *and* down tree branches and trunks. It wedges nuts into cracks in tree bark and uses its long, dagger-shaped beak to hammer them open. Look out for nuthatches in oak and beech woods.

WOODLAND BIRDS

TREE HOMES

Both broad-leaved and coniferous trees provide homes for woodland birds. Learn which birds to look for where.

◀ Oaks are home for chiffchaffs, tawny owls, blackcaps, woodpeckers, willow warblers, and many more.

◀ Scots pines are less popular, but still attract siskins, woodpigeons, goldcrests, spotted flycatchers, and others.

coniferous or evergreen trees, which keep their leaves all year. Woodland which contains a mixture of these should provide the biggest variety of birds for you to see.

Each type of tree is home to different insects and provides different seeds or nuts. Birds have adapted to feed on these various trees and many bird species will be found in one type of tree.

Oak is one of the best trees for birds. Large numbers of insects can be found on its leaves and hiding in its bark crevices. The insects are food for both resident birds and summer visitors. Oaks also produce acorns, much liked by jays and woodpigeons. Jays hide acorns by burying them in

▶ **One-way Trip**
Unlike the nuthatch, the treecreeper rarely climbs down trees. It usually starts at the bottom of a tree and climbs up and around the trunk. Treecreepers love to eat insects and use their thin beaks to poke them out of cracks in trees.

WOODLAND BIRDS

FOREST FOOD

Woodland provides a wide variety of foods for birds. Trees and bushes provide nuts and berries. Insects are attracted to the trees, and their grubs, such as caterpillars, are particular favourites for hungry birds.

▲ Jays love acorns. They often bury some in the ground to eat later.

▲ Caterpillars are the main spring and summer food of tits.

▲ Greenfly, which are tree pests, are avidly eaten by birds.

▲ In the autumn when insects are scarce, many birds eat fruit such as elderberries as well.

the ground, and in this way they help new trees to grow.

Alder and birch trees have small seeds. Small birds like siskins, which have sharply pointed beaks, feed at these trees. Ash has larger seeds, so it attracts birds like the bullfinch because it has a stouter beak.

Beech trees produce large quantities of seeds, or beech mast, every few years. This is important winter food for tits and finches.

Pine and spruce trees are coniferous and keep their leaves

▶ **Tell-Tale Signs**
These children have spotted evidence of a woodland bird. Their photographs will give them a record they can check at home using a field guide.

▼ **Warm Nest**
This female woodpigeon keeps her eggs warm in this typical nest made of twigs. The incubation period will last 17–19 days.

WATCH THE BIRDIE!

When you are experienced at identifying birds, it can be fun to take photographs to illustrate your notes. It is very difficult to photograph birds in flight or to get close enough to photograph them standing still. Instead, take pictures of their abandoned nests, habitats or stray feathers.

through the winter. You should find goldcrests, coal tits, and siskins around them.

Woodlands with lots of foreign coniferous trees, such as Sitka spruce, do not attract the insects that birds eat, but starlings, thrushes, and finches may roost in them.

WOODLAND NESTS

Dead trees provide a good place to look for birds. An old, decaying trunk will contain grubs and insects which attract birds. The soft wood also makes it easy for woodpeckers to prepare a nest hole. Tits also nest in stumps or broken branches.

Many woodland birds prefer trees to build their nests in, using the branches or tree holes. Tits, redstarts, and nuthatches prefer old trees for their nest sites. Sadly for them, most trees are now cut down by forest owners or managers before they become very old. Other birds like to nest on the ground or in vegetation.

▶ **Feed Me!**
A hungry green woodpecker chick sticks its beak out of the nest, hoping to be fed.

▼ **Starling Supper**
This sparrowhawk uses its long, sharp talons to snatch its supper: a starling.

BIRD CALLS AND SONGS

Recognizing the sounds birds make is very important. A bird's call and song are two of the best clues to its identity.

Practise writing the noises birds make. Use letters which sound like the noise, and add lines above them to indicate if the sound rises or falls. Curving lines indicate a more gradual change.

Treecreeper song
tsee-tsee-tsee-sissi-sissi-sweee

Goldcrest call
zee-zee-zee

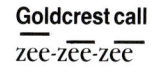

Green woodpecker song
keu-keu-keu

Woodpigeon song
coo-cooo-cooo-coo-coo

Chiffchaff song
chiff-chaff, chiff-chiff-chaff

Visit the wood at different times of day and various times of year. Make a note of which birds are singing and when. Count how many times a bird sings in a specific period, such as 5 minutes. You will begin to see a pattern for each species. Most birds sing in the early morning and again in the evening.

WOODLAND BIRDS

SPARROW-HAWK
Accipiter nisus

Beak and bright yellow eye

Appearance A small bird of prey with rounded wings, a long tail, and a bright yellow eye. The male is grey above and has pale under-parts with orange bars. The larger female is brown above with dark brown bars below. The tail has dark bands across it.
Habits Likes wooded country with conifers. When hunting it flies fast along the edge of trees or hedges to catch prey by surprise. Often soars high with occasional wing flaps.
Status Resident.
Size Male 30 cm (12 in) Female 38 cm (15 in)
Weight Male 150 g (5⅓ oz) Female 300 g (11 oz)
Call A harsh 'kek-kek-kek'
Nest Twigs, sometimes in an old nest of another bird.
Nest site In a tree, near the trunk.
Eggs 3–5, bluish-white with brown blotches. 1 brood.
Incubation 33–35 days
First flight 24–30 days
Food Small birds, some mammals, and insects.

Sparrowhawk

Tawny owl

TAWNY OWL
Strix aluco

Appearance Bulky, large-headed, and brown with a round face and large eyes. Broad, dark rounded wings.
Habits Active at night. More often heard than seen. Roosts on a tree hole or close to the trunk during the day. Hunts in or near woods.
Status Resident.

Fourth claw can swivel backwards.

Size 38 cm (15 in)
Weight 330–440 g (12–16 oz)
Call A hooting 'hoo-hoo, hoo, hooo-ooo-ooo' and a sharp 'ke-wick'.
Nest Does not build a nest.
Nest site Uses a hole in a tree, sometimes in the old nest of another bird.
Eggs 2–3, white. 1 brood.
Incubation 28–30 days
First flight 32–37 days
Food Mainly small mammals and birds.

WOODLAND BIRDS

Turtle Dove
Streptopelia turtur

Appearance Slim with a long, white-edged tail. Has a grey head and neck and grey-brown back and tail. The wings are reddish-brown with black spots, the breast is pink and the belly pale.

Wing feather with red-brown edge

Habits Flies rapidly, flicking its wings. Found in woodland, parks, and open country with hedges.

Status Summer visitor.
Size 27 cm (10¾ in)
Weight 100–150 g (3½–5⅓ oz)
Song A purring 'rroorrrr'.
Nest Flimsy platform of twigs.
Nest site Bushes and hedges.
Eggs 2, white. 2 broods.
Incubation 13–14 days
First flight 20–21 days
Food Seeds and leaves.

Turtle dove

Woodpigeon

Woodpigeon
Columba palumbus

Appearance A large, grey bird with a small head and long tail. Has grey upper parts, a purple-brown breast and pale belly. The adult has a white neck patch and white on the wings.

Beak and pale-coloured eye

Habits Likes woods and copses, as well as parks and gardens. Feeds in fields, often in flocks. When disturbed it flies off with clattering wings. Can breed as late as November.
Status Resident.
Size 41 cm (16½ in)
Weight 450–520 g (16–18½ oz)
Song A hoarse 'coo-cooo-cooo-coo-coo'.
Nest Simply built, using small twigs.
Nest site Hedges or trees.
Eggs 2, white. 2 broods.
Incubation 17–19 days
First flight 16–34 days
Food Grains, leaves, seeds, berries, and some insects.

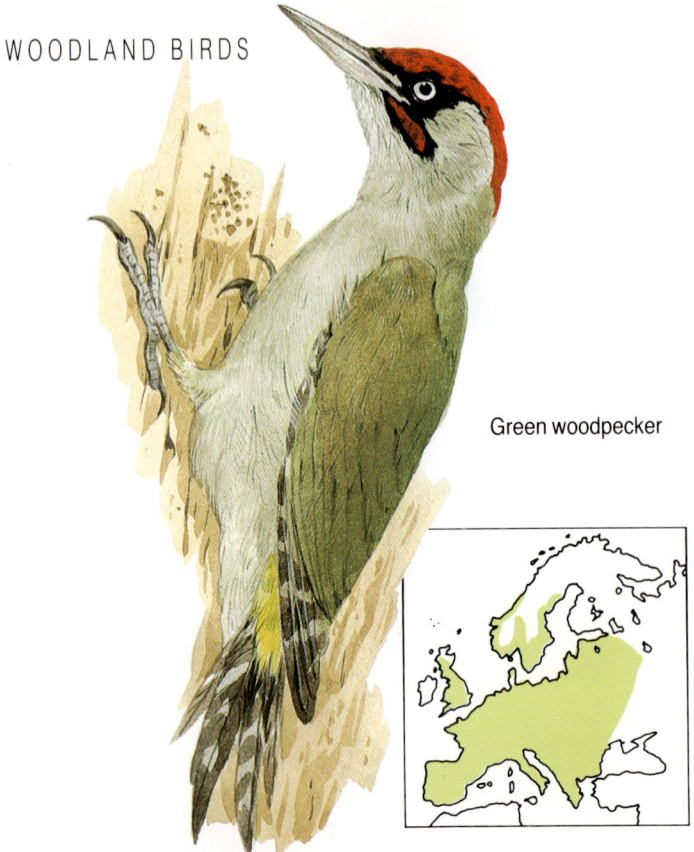

WOODLAND BIRDS

Green woodpecker

GREEN WOODPECKER
Picus viridis

Appearance A short-tailed bird with a strong beak. Has green upper parts and pale under-parts, with a red crown, a black face, and a yellow rump in flight.

Forward- and backward-pointing toes

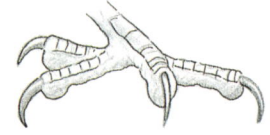

Habits Found in deciduous woodland and parks, where it climbs up tree trunks and branches. Flies with rapid wing-beats, closing wings occasionally to give a bouncing flight. Feeds on the ground and on trees.
Status Resident.
Size 32 cm (12¾ in)
Weight 180–220 g (6½–7¾ oz)
Call Ringing laugh – 'keu-keu-keu'.
Nest Lining of a few wood chips.
Nest site Hole excavated in a tree.
Eggs 5–7, white. 1 brood.
Incubation 17–19 days
First flight 23–27 days
Food Insects, especially ants.

Long tongue for catching ants

GREAT SPOTTED WOODPECKER
Dendrocopos major

Appearance A short-tailed, black and white bird. The upper parts are black with white shoulder patches. The under-parts are white with red under the tail. The head is patterned with black and white. The male has a red patch on the back of the head and the young have a red crown.

Habits Found in mixed woodland, parks, and large gardens, where it climbs up tree trunks and branches. Feeds in trees but will visit bird tables for peanuts. Announces its territory with loud drumming of its beak on a branch. Flies with a bouncy flight.
Status Resident.
Size 23 cm (9 in)
Weight 70–90 g (2½–3 oz)

Stiff, spiny tail feathers

Call A sharp 'tchik'. Drums rapidly on trees with beak.
Nest Lining of wood chips.
Nest site Hole in a tree.
Eggs 4–7, white. 1 brood.
Incubation 15–16 days
First flight 20–24 days
Food Insects, spiders, nuts, and seeds.

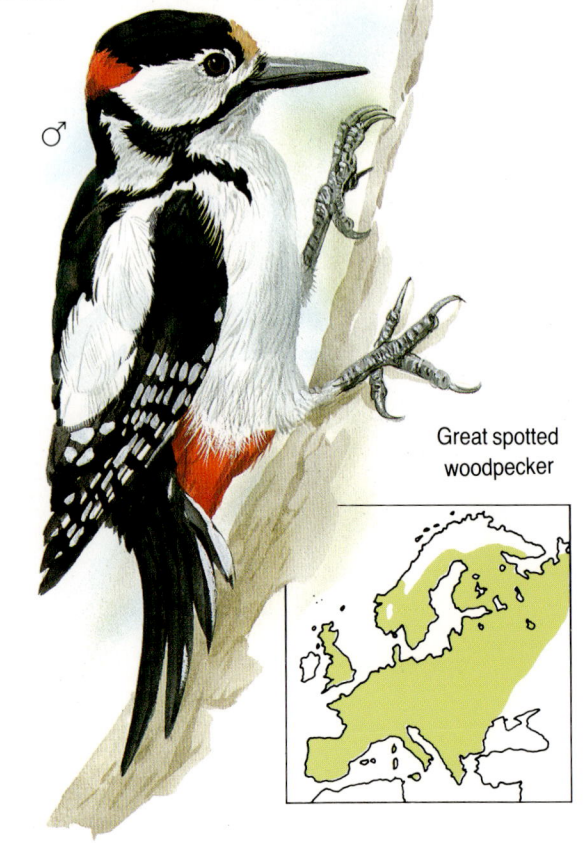

♂

Great spotted woodpecker

WOODLAND BIRDS

WILLOW WARBLER
Phylloscopus trochilus

Autumn colouring

Appearance A small bird with a greenish-brown back and pale yellow under-parts that turn bright yellow in autumn. Has a pale stripe above eye and pale brown legs. Young birds have bright yellow under-parts.
Habits Always active, flitting through the leaves or searching branches for insects. Likes woodland but also found in open areas with hedges.
Status Summer visitor.
Size 11 cm (4½ in)
Weight 6–10 g (⅕–⅓ oz)
Song A warbling series of notes descending and finishing with a flourish.
Call A plaintive 'hoo-weet'.
Nest A domed nest of moss and grass lined with feathers.
Nest site On or near the ground in the bottom of bushes and hedges.
Eggs 6 or 7, white with red spots. 1 brood.
Incubation 13 days
First flight 13–14 days
Food Insects and spiders.

Willow warbler

Chiffchaff

CHIFFCHAFF
Phylloscopus collybita

Appearance A small bird with brown upper parts and buffish under-parts – duller than the willow warbler. Has a pale stripe above each eye and dark legs. Young birds have yellowish under-parts.
Habits Very active, constantly flicking wings and tail while searching for food in trees. Will dart and hover to catch insects in flight. Likes woods with thick undergrowth.
Status Summer visitor, some spend the winter.
Size 11 cm (4½ in)
Weight 6–9 g (⅕–⅓ oz)
Song A distinctive 'chiff-chaff, chiff-chiff-chaff'.
Call A soft 'hweet'.
Nest Domed and made of leaves, grass, and moss lined with feathers.
Nest site Usually just above the ground in a bush or brambles.
Eggs 5 or 6, white with reddish-brown spots. 1 or 2 broods.
Incubation 13 days
First flight 13–14 days
Food Insects.

Hovering before catching insects

WOODLAND BIRDS

BLACKCAP
Sylvia atricapilla

Appearance Fairly slim with grey-brown upper parts, greyish under-parts, and a long tail. The male has a black cap and the female and young have a reddish-brown one.
Habits Actively feeds in trees and bushes. Likes open woodland and overgrown areas with plenty of trees.
Status Summer visitor, some spend the winter.
Size 14 cm (5½ in)
Weight 14–20 g (about ⅗ oz)
Song A clear, short, and rich warble.
Call A hard 'tacc, tacc'.
Nest A cup of stems and grass lined with fine grass and hair.
Nest site Low in hedges, brambles, and nettles.
Eggs 4 or 5, pale with dark brown spots. 1 or 2 broods.
Incubation 10–12 days
First flight 10–13 days
Food Insects, fruit, and berries.

Male eating an elderberry

Blackcap

GARDEN WARBLER
Sylvia borin

Appearance A plump, brown and buff bird with no distinctive markings. The beak and tail are short and the eyes dark.
Habits Active, but keeps well hidden among leaves. Likes open woodland with bushes and brambles.
Status Summer visitor.
Size 14 cm (5½ in)
Weight 16–23 g (about ⅔ oz)
Song A rich, prolonged warbling, faster and quieter than the blackcap.
Call A hard 'tacc, tacc'.

Garden warbler

Garden warbler in song

Nest A cup of grass lined with fine grass and hair.
Nest site In shrubs and brambles.
Eggs 4 or 5, pale with dark spots. 1 brood.
Incubation 12 days
First flight 9–12 days
Food Insects, spiders, and berries.

WOODLAND BIRDS

GOLDCREST
Regulus regulus

Appearance A very small, plump bird with a short tail and a fine beak. Has dull green upper parts and pale grey under-parts with pale bars on the wings. The male has a yellow and orange crown stripe, edged with black. The crown feathers are spread to show the orange during display. The female's crown is yellow and black.
Habits Very active, flitting, hovering, and hanging to find food. Likes coniferous woods and gardens. Often joins flocks of tits in winter.
Status Resident.
Size 9 cm (3½ in)
Weight 5–7 g (about ⅕ oz)
Song A very high repeated note ending with a flourish.
Call Thin 'zee-zee-zee'.
Nest A deep cup of moss and spiders' webs lined with feathers.
Nest site Usually hanging from a conifer branch.
Eggs 7 or 8, white with brown spots. 2 broods.
Incubation 16 days
First flight 18–20 days
Food Spiders and insects.

Male's display colouring

SPOTTED FLYCATCHER
Muscicapa striata

Appearance Grey-brown with white under-parts and brown breast streaks. The crown is streaked with dark brown and the beak is small and flat with bristles around the base.
Habits Likes open woodland, parks, and gardens. Perches very upright on an open perch. Flies out to catch insects with an audible snap of its beak.
Status Summer visitor.
Size 14 cm (5½ in)

Bristles around the beak

Weight 13–19 g (about ½ oz)
Song Sequence of 6 high, squeaky notes.
Call A thin 'tsee' or 'tsee-chuk'.
Nest A cup of moss, hair, and cobwebs with a finer lining.
Nest site In vegetation against a wall or a tree trunk. Will use open-fronted nest box.
Eggs 4 or 5, greenish-blue with red blotches. 2 broods.
Incubation 12–14 days
First flight 12–15 days
Food Insects caught in flight.

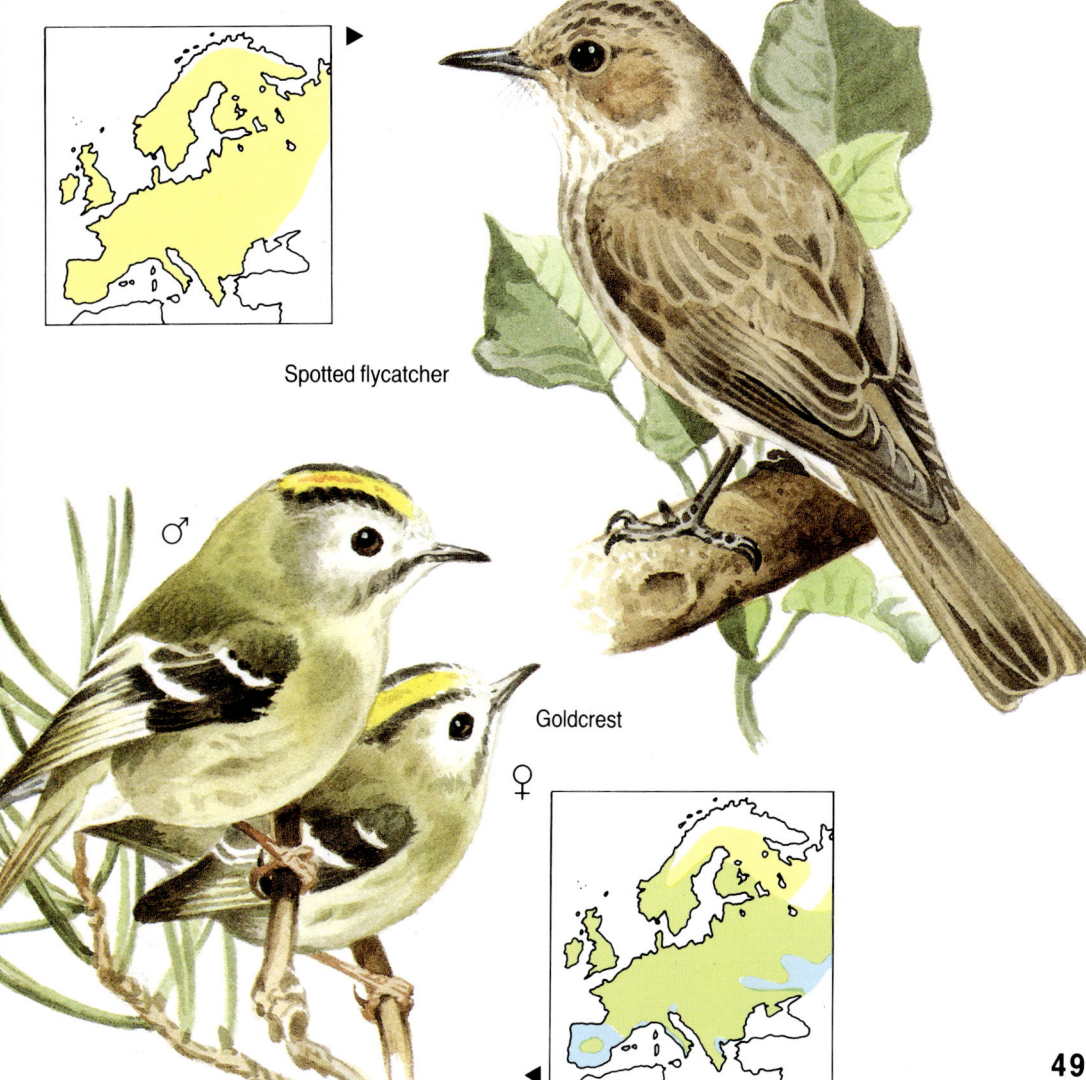

Spotted flycatcher

Goldcrest

♂ ♀

49

WOODLAND BIRDS

JAY
Garrulus glandarius

Wing colouring

Appearance A brownish-pink body with a white rump and black tail. Has a white forehead with dark streaks, a large black 'moustache' and black wings with a large blue patch.

Habits Likes woodland, parks, and gardens. Flapping flight with rounded wings. Often noisy. It spends a lot of time in trees but also hops on the ground. Buries any acorns it does not eat.
Status Resident.
Size 34 cm (13½ in)
Weight 140–190 g (5–7 oz)
Call Loud, shrieking 'kaaak'.
Nest Made of sticks, twigs, and earth lined with roots.
Nest site Low in a tree or in a tall bush.
Eggs 5 or 6, greenish with small brown spots. 1 brood.
Incubation 16 days
First flight 20 days
Food Nuts and fruit, especially acorns. Also insects, spiders, and birds' eggs.

Jay

LONG-TAILED TIT
Aegithalos caudatus

Appearance A tiny black and white, long-tailed bird. Has a black back and tail with a pink patch on the body and white underparts. The white head has a black stripe along the side.

Tail feather

Habits Found in open woodland and hedges. Very active and often in large flocks. Hangs from branches when searching for food.

Hanging from a twig

Status Resident.
Size 14 cm (5½ in). The tail is about 7 cm (2¾ in).
Weight 7–9 g (¼–⅓ oz)
Call A trilling 'tsirrp' and high 'zee-zee-zee'.
Nest Ball-shaped, made of moss, cobwebs, hair, and lichens and lined with feathers.
Nest site Thick bush – brambles or hawthorn.
Eggs 7–12, white with small red specks. 1 brood.
Incubation 13–14 days
First flight 15–16 days
Food Insects, spiders, and some seeds.

Long-tailed tit

50

WOODLAND BIRDS

Marsh Tit
Parus palustris

Seed-eating beak

Appearance A small bird with a brown back, white under-parts, and a small beak. The head has a glossy black cap and bib with white cheeks.
Habits Likes deciduous woods and hedges. Does not feed high in trees and often joins feeding flocks. Hangs from branches.
Status Resident.
Size 11.5 cm (4½ in)
Weight 9–12 g (about ⅜ oz)
Song A series of repeated notes – 'chip, chip . . .' or 'chippi, chippi . . .'.
Call A loud 'pitchou', a harsh 'tcha', and 'chicka-dee-dee-dee'.
Nest Moss lined with hair.
Nest site A hole in a tree.
Eggs 6–8, white with red spots. 1 brood.
Incubation 13 days
First flight 16–18 days
Food Insects, seeds, and berries.

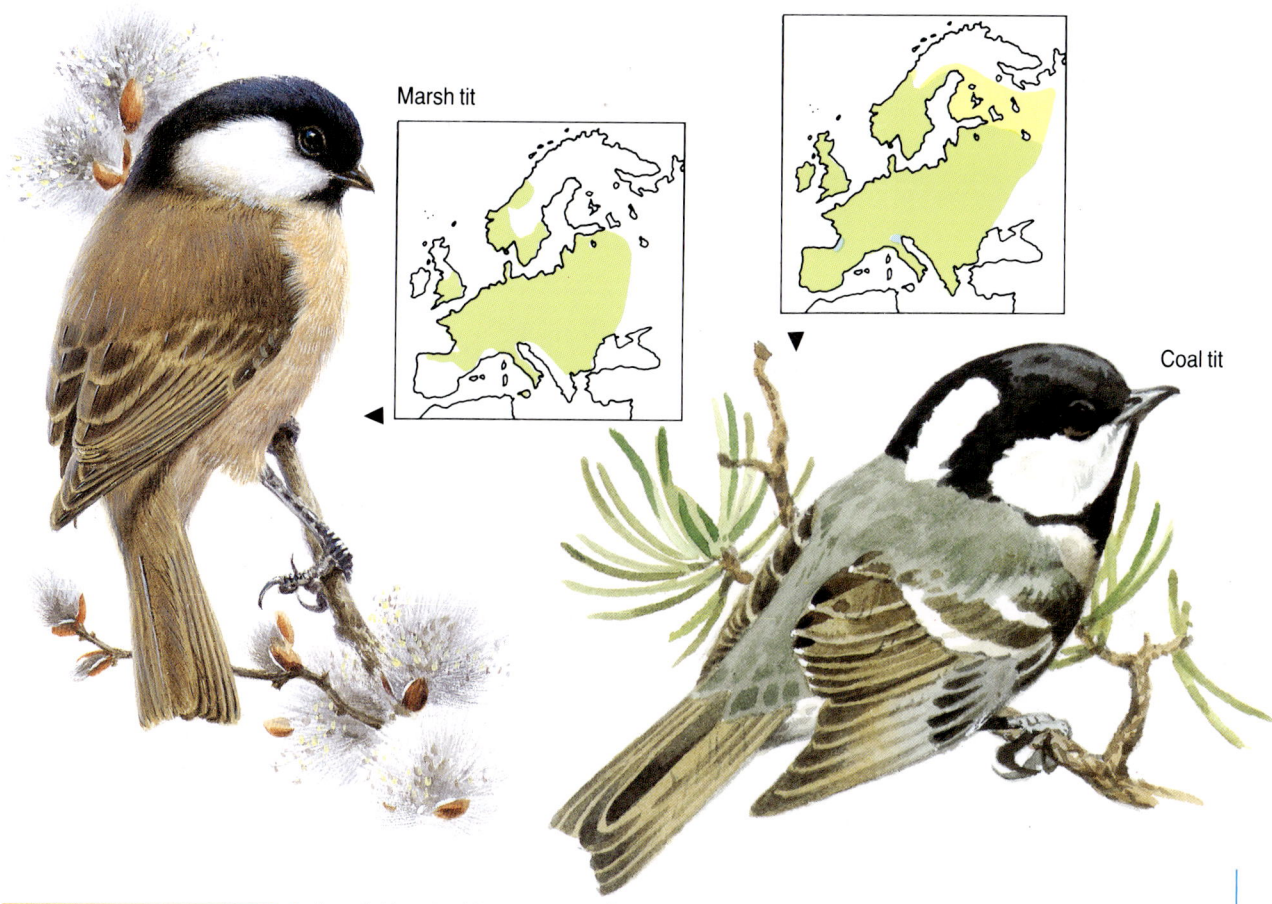

Marsh tit

Coal tit

Coal Tit
Parus ater

Appearance A small, grey and white bird with a black cap and a large black bib, white cheeks, and a white patch on the back of its head. Has 2 white wing bars. The young are slightly yellowish.
Habits Found in woods and gardens, particularly in conifers. Feeds in branches and on tree trunks. Forms flocks with other tits.
Status Resident.
Size 11.5 cm (4½ in)
Weight 8–10 g (about ⅓ oz)
Song A piping 'see-too, see-too, see-too'.
Call A plaintive 'tseu' and a high 'zee-zee-zee'.
Nest Moss lined with hair.
Nest site A hole in a bank or tree stump.
Eggs 7–11, white with red spots. 1 brood.
Incubation 14 days
First flight 16–19 days
Food Insects, seeds, and nuts. Often hides food.

Clinging to the side of a tree trunk

WOODLAND BIRDS

TREECREEPER
Certhia familiaris

Foot with long curved claws

Appearance A small, mouse-like bird with mottled brown upper parts and white under-parts. Has a whitish stripe above the eye, thin and down-curved beak, and a pointed tail.
Habits Found in fairly mature, mainly deciduous, woodland, parks, and gardens. Climbs up tree trunks and along branches, often on the underside. Joins flocks of tits in winter.
Status Resident. The similar short-toed treecreeper is also found in mainland Europe.
Size 12.5 cm (5 in)
Weight 8–12 g (about ⅓ oz)
Song A series of high, descending notes ending with a flourish.
Call High, loud 'tsee'.
Nest Twigs, moss, and grass lined with feathers and wool.
Nest site In cracks in a tree trunk or behind an ivy stem.
Eggs 5 or 6, white with reddish spots. 1 or 2 broods.
Incubation 14–15 days
First flight 14–15 days
Food Mainly insects.

Treecreeper

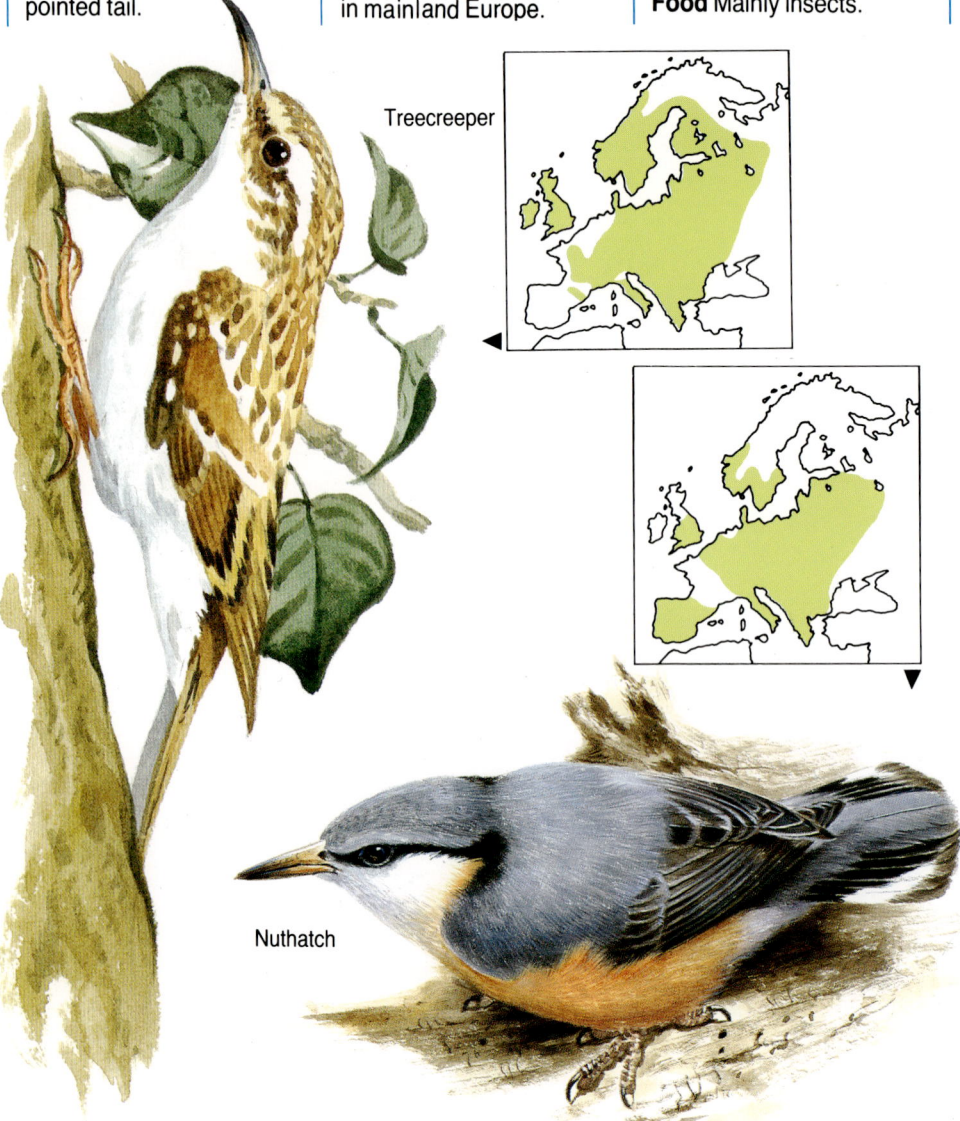

NUTHATCH
Sitta europaea

Appearance A plump, short-tailed bird with a dagger-shaped beak. Has blue-grey upper parts and buff-orange under-parts, a black stripe through the eye, and white cheeks and throat.
Habits Likes woods, parks, and gardens with old deciduous trees. Climbs up and down tree trunks with ease. Hammers nuts with its sharp beak.
Status Resident.
Size 14 cm (5½ in)
Weight 19–24 g (about ¾ oz)
Song A loud 'quee-quee-quee' and rapid trilling.
Call A loud 'chwit-chwit-chwit' and a high, repeated 'tsit'.
Nest A layer of bark flakes.
Nest site A hole in a tree trunk or branch or a hole-fronted nest box. The entrance is plastered with mud.
Eggs 5–8, white with red spots. 1 brood.
Incubation 14–15 days
First flight 23–25 days
Food Nuts, seeds, and insects.

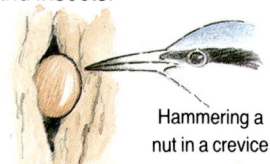

Nuthatch

Hammering a nut in a crevice

WOODLAND BIRDS

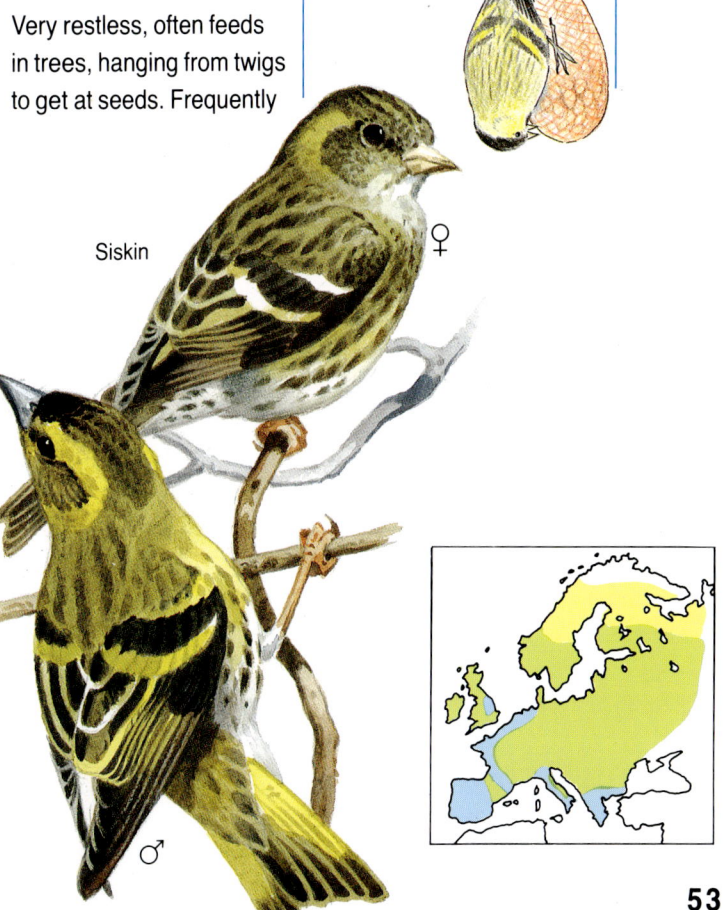

BULLFINCH
Pyrrhula pyrrhula

Appearance A stout bird with a black cap, grey back, black wings with a white wing bar, white rump, and black tail. The male has bright pink-red cheeks and under-parts. The female has buff-pink cheeks and under-parts. The young are like the female but without the black cap.
Habits Likes woods, thickets, hedges, and orchards. Usually found in pairs or small groups. Flight is slow and slightly bouncing.
Status Resident.
Size 15 cm (6 in)
Weight 22–27 g (¾–1 oz)
Song A short, quiet warble.
Call A soft piping 'deu'.
Nest A cup of twigs and moss lined with roots.
Nest site In a thick bush or hedge.
Eggs 4–6, pale blue with dark spots. 2 broods.
Incubation 12–14 days
First flight 12–16 days
Food Seeds, berries, buds, and insects.

Young bullfinch's colouring

SISKIN
Carduelis spinus

Appearance A small, streaky, yellow-green bird with a sharp beak, forked tail and dark wings with 2 yellow wing bars. The male has a black crown and chin. The female has a streaked crown and less yellow.
Habits Likes coniferous woodland for breeding, and birch and alder in winter. Very restless, often feeds in trees, hanging from twigs to get at seeds. Frequently found in large, noisy flocks.
Status Resident and winter visitor.
Size 12 cm (4¾ in)
Weight 10–14 g (about ½ oz)
Song A twittering warble.
Call A clear 'tsu'.
Nest A small cup of twigs and moss lined with feathers.
Nest site High in conifer trees.
Eggs 4–5, pale blue with reddish spots. 2 broods.
Incubation 11–12 days
First flight 15 days
Food Mainly seeds. Peanuts at a bird table.

Hanging on a nut feeder

Open Country and Upland Birds

If you are patient and stay very still and quiet, open fields can provide good views of birds feeding and of large flocks in winter.

Sadly, modern farming methods have caused the disappearance of many hedgerows, bushes, and rough grassy areas at the edge of fields. This means there are fewer birds, as they no longer have so many places to nest and to feed. The use of chemical pesticides to kill insects and weeds in fields also means there is less food for birds, too.

Modern farming methods have also encouraged the use of huge

▲ **Rough and Rugged**
Stark, rugged countryside is home to many birds. The few trees provide roosts, while the bushes and other plants are sources of food and shelter.

▲ **Autumn Arrival**
Each autumn, large, noisy flocks of fieldfares arrive in Britain for the winter. They find wild fruits, berries, insects, and snails to eat in the open countryside. You will often see fieldfares in flocks with redwings, another species of thrush.

OPEN COUNTRY AND UPLAND BIRDS

◀ **Fresh Food**
Birds flock around farmers ploughing fields because there are worms to eat in the newly turned soil. Traditional feeding grounds, such as hedgerows, have now become scarce.

FIELD FEAST

Rabbits, mice, rats, and voles are food for kestrels (below). Buzzards eat rabbits and birds, as well as the remains of dead animals.

fields containing just one crop. This means that fields of suitable food may now be quite a distance apart, making it difficult for young birds to find new areas where they can establish themselves.

Pied wagtails, for example, have become less common where grass fields have been converted to wheat or other crops, and farm ponds have been filled in. These birds continue to thrive in areas where fields are bordered by stone walls, which provide ideal nesting places. You will be able to find the pied wagtails' roost by following the birds at dusk.

If you count the birds at the roost regularly, you should notice numbers building up in the winter. This is because, as roosts become established in the autumn, more birds learn where they are and join.

The hedgerows that remain in the countryside, however, provide good places to watch birds. Small birds can move across fields by hopping from one to another, without being seen by predators such as the kestrel or sparrowhawk.

Many open country birds flock together. This provides protection because it makes it difficult for a

OPEN COUNTRY AND UPLAND BIRDS

predator to snatch an individual bird or sneak up unseen. When the flock finds a source of food all the birds eat quickly and fly off together.

FINDING FOOD

Seeds provide food for many open country birds in the autumn and winter, and some eat insects in the spring and summer. Swallows, however, can only eat insects. This is why they migrate south to search for food when the cold weather starts.

The kestrel is the most common bird of prey you will see in open countryside. It can usually be found hovering beside a road, watching for its next meal of a mouse, rat, or vole. Buzzards are larger and less common. They are usually seen circling over trees.

Field animals like small voles also provide food for short-eared owls. Voles sometimes have population explosions. When this happens, the owls also have more young.

DOWNS, MOORS, AND HEATHS

Open grass downland is home for a wide variety of birds including

▲ **Good Mover**
The pied wagtail gets its name from the way it constantly wags its tail as it walks and runs along the ground. In the summer it likes heaths and moors, where it finds an abundant supply of insects, spiders, and worms to eat.

▲ **Looking Good**
It is easy to identify a lapwing by its long crest. Most lapwings leave their upland breeding grounds in autumn to spend winter in lower or more southerly areas. They live in large flocks in the winter, often with golden plovers. Noisy and active, they can put on acrobatic displays in flight.

ON THE WATCH

Birds have extremely good vision. They cannot move their eyes very much, so move their heads instead. Many have eyes on the side of their head, but birds of prey and owls have their eyes facing forwards.

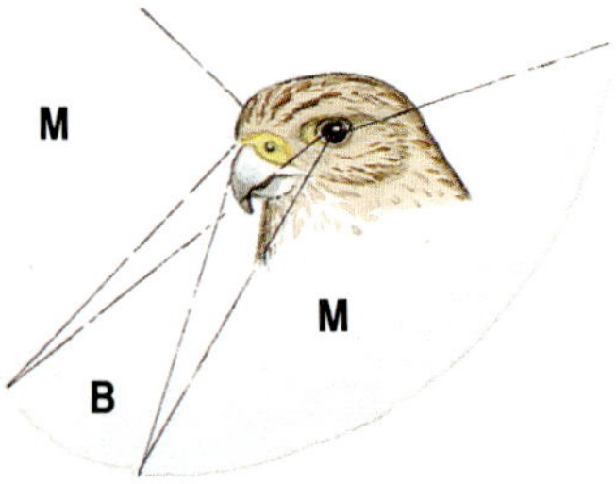

► **Kestrel**
The kestrel's forward-facing eyes give it good binocular vision (vision using both eyes together). This enables it to judge distances and catch prey.

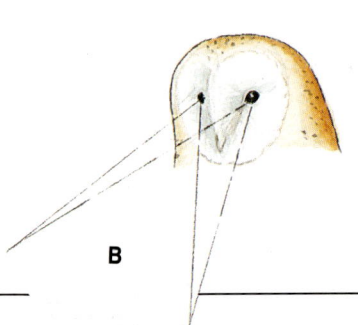

▼ **Owl**
Owls can see well in daylight as well as at night. They pinpoint their prey using hearing as well as binocular vision.

OPEN COUNTRY AND UPLAND BIRDS

◀ **Meadow Meal**
Meadow pipits feed on juicy worms, as well as insects, spiders, and seeds. Look out for these birds not only in meadows but also on downs and moors.

skylarks, lapwings, meadow pipits, and grey partridges. Nearby bushes and hedges attract yellowhammers and linnets. Trees provide nesting places for rooks, kestrels, and goldfinches. Bushes and grassy areas are where cuckoos search for nests. You may see cuckoos being chased by smaller birds trying to protect their nests.

Lowland moors and heaths with their covering of heather, gorse, and rough grass provide ideal breeding and feeding areas for linnets, yellowhammers, skylarks, and meadow pipits. Gorse bushes provide safe nesting sites because the prickly leaves protect the nests and young from predators. Hawthorn bushes, with their hard thorns, are also safe places for birds to breed. They have the advantage of producing berries for food during winter, too. Northern moors are also home to golden plovers and lapwings (see page 60), dunlins and curlews (see pages 88–89).

Upland moors are the breeding grounds for many unusual birds, such as hen harriers, merlins, ring ousels, and twites. Buzzards, golden plovers, and short-eared owls also like these areas. Sadly, a great deal of moorland and its wildlife has been lost to sheep grazing and the planting of conifer trees.

CRAFTY CUCKOO

The cuckoo lays its eggs in the nests of other birds – usually reed warblers or meadow pipits. When the cuckoo hatches, it pushes the host bird's eggs out of the nest (above), usually leaving the parents with just one outsize chick (below)!

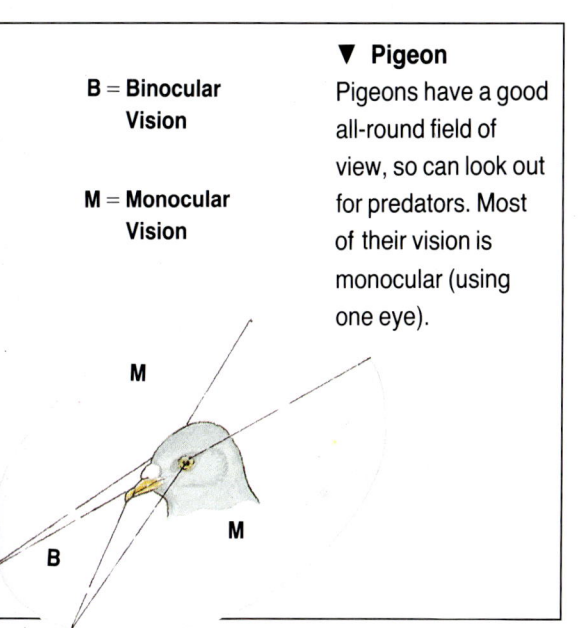

B = **Binocular Vision**

M = **Monocular Vision**

▼ **Pigeon**
Pigeons have a good all-round field of view, so can look out for predators. Most of their vision is monocular (using one eye).

57

OPEN COUNTRY AND UPLAND BIRDS

KESTREL
Falco tinnunculus

Appearance The male has a grey head, chestnut back with black spots, and a grey tail. His under-parts are buff with dark streaks. The female is brown all over. The tail is long with pointed wings.

Hooked beak

Habits Found in open country and in towns. Often seen along roadsides, hovering in search of food. Also perches on telephone wires and posts.
Status Resident. This is the most common bird of prey in Europe.
Size 34 cm (13½ in). The wing-span is 75 cm (30 in).
Weight Male 200–240 g (7–8½ oz). Female 220–300 g (7¾–11 oz).
Call A loud 'kee-kee-kee'.
Nest No material used.
Nest site A hole in a tree, cliff face, or building. Sometimes uses an old crow's nest.
Eggs 3–6, white with red-brown blotches. 1 brood.
Incubation 27–29 days
First flight 27–32 days
Food Small mammals and birds and some insects.

BUZZARD
Buteo buteo

Appearance A large brown bird of prey with rounded wings and a short, broad tail. Often has contrasting dark and light areas under the wings.

Talons for grabbing prey

Habits Often perches on posts and telephone poles. May be seen on the ground walking awkwardly. Soars with wings and tail spread.
Status Resident.
Size 54 cm (21½ in). The wing-span is 120 cm (48 in).

Soaring with wings and tail spread

Weight Male 550–850 g (1¼–2 lb). Female 700–1200 g (1½–2⅔ lb).
Call A mewing 'peeooo'.
Nest Twigs and branches.
Nest site In a tree or on a rocky ledge.
Eggs 2–4, white with red-brown blotches. 1 brood.
Incubation 36–38 days
First flight 50–55 days
Food Small mammals, especially rabbits, and some birds. Also feeds on dead animals and scavenges.

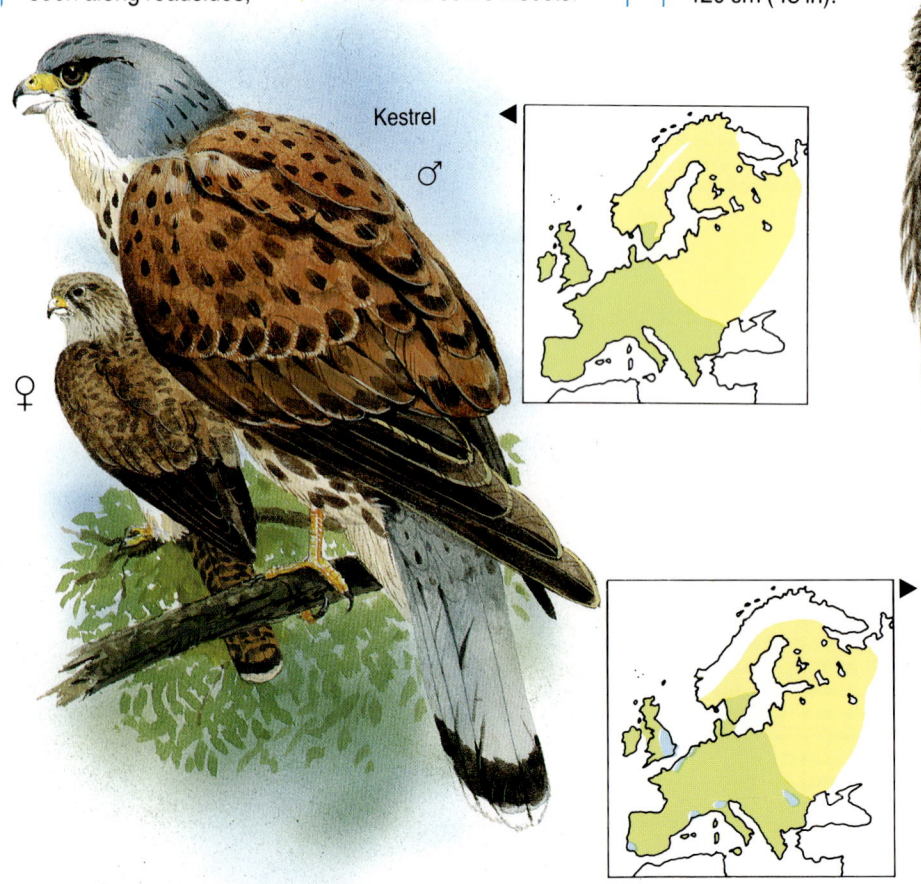

Kestrel ♂
♀

Buzzard

58

OPEN COUNTRY AND UPLAND BIRDS

Pheasant

Grey partridge

♂ ♀

PHEASANT
Phasianus colchicus

Appearance Large with a long tail. The male is highly coloured with a blue-green head, red skin on the face, and copper-coloured body and tail. There are dark bars across the tail. The female is brown with a shorter tail.

Colourful tail feather

Habits It usually runs or crouches if disturbed. Flies with rapid wing-beats or glides, often bursting noisily from cover. Can be tame if artificially reared.
Status Resident.
Size Male up to 89 cm (35½ in).
Female up to 63 cm (25 in).
Weight 900–1400 g (2–3 lb)
Call A loud 'karrk-karrk'.
Nest Lined with grass and leaves.
Nest site A hollow on the ground in thick grass or under hedges and bushes.
Eggs 8–15, olive-brown. 1 brood.
Incubation 22–28 days
First flight 14 days. Full-grown at 70–80 days.
Food Roots, leaves, seeds, and grains.

GREY PARTRIDGE
Perdix perdix

Appearance A dumpy bird with short wings and a short, rounded tail. Has an orange face, streaked brown back, and chestnut tail. Grey breast and pale under-parts with a horseshoe-shaped dark brown mark. Grey legs.

Covey on ground

Wing colouring

Habits Found in open fields of grass and crops, often in small groups or coveys. When disturbed, flies low for short distances with rapid wing-beats.
Status Resident.
Size 34 cm (13½ in)
Weight 350–450 g (12½–16 oz)
Call A loud, high 'kerr-ic, kerr-ic', like a creaky gate.
Nest Lined with dry grasses and leaves.
Nest site On the ground in a hollow at the bottom of hedges or bushes.
Eggs 10–20, olive-brown. 1 brood.
Incubation 23–25 days
First flight About 16 days. Full grown at 90–100 days.
Food Seeds, grains, and vegetable matter.

OPEN COUNTRY AND UPLAND BIRDS

LAPWING
Vanellus vanellus

Male's winter colouring

Appearance Has round wings with a distinctive long crest on its head. The back and wings are dark green and the throat and breast are black. The sides of the face, neck, and under-parts are white. Looks black and white in flight. Has white chin and throat in winter.
Habits Likes open country and uplands. Flies with slow wing-beats, tumbling and twisting in display flight. Walks or runs, then pauses before moving again. Found in fields in large flocks during winter.
Status Resident and winter visitor.
Size 30 cm (12 in)
Weight 150–310 g (5⅓–11½ oz)
Song Given in flight – 'peerweet, weet-weet, peerweet'.
Call A shrill 'pee-wit'.
Nest A muddy hollow lined with grass.
Nest site In short plants.
Eggs 4, pale brown with black blotches. 1 brood.
Incubation 26–28 days
First flight Runs at once and flies after 5–6 weeks.
Food Snails, insects, worms, and seeds.

Lapwing

GOLDEN PLOVER
Pluvialis apricaria

Appearance Has gold- and black-spangled upper parts. The under-parts are black in summer and white in winter. Stands upright.
Habits Runs and then stops before running again. In summer it perches on rocks and knolls to keep watch. In winter it forms flocks in fields.
Status Resident, passage migrant, and winter visitor.
Size 28 cm (11¼ in)
Weight 140–210 g (5–7½ oz)
Song A sad 'trr-peeoo' in display flight.
Call A whistling 'tluii'.
Nest A slight hollow with a few twigs.
Nest site Among heather.
Eggs 4, buff with black spots. 1 brood.
Incubation 28–30 days
First flight Leaves nest immediately and flies after 4 weeks.
Food Insects, snails, worms, and some seeds.

Golden plover

Different breeding plumage of northern race (left) and southern race

OPEN COUNTRY AND UPLAND BIRDS

SHORT-EARED OWL
Asio flammeus

Appearance Pale brown and mottled with darker brown on the back and dark streaks below. Has a pale face with dark-bordered, bright yellow eyes and small ear-tufts. Has long wings in flight with a dark patch at the front of them.

Facial disc and eyes

Habits Feeds during the day, and is often seen flying over rough grasslands, marshes, and moors. Usually lands on the ground but can also land on posts or bushes.
Status Resident and winter visitor.
Size 38 cm (15 in)
Weight 260–310 g (9–11½ oz)
Call A barking 'kwowk' and a low 'hoo-hoo-hoo'.
Nest A rough hollow.

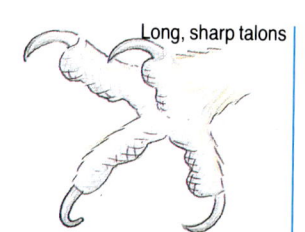

Long, sharp talons

Nest site On the ground in heather, gorse, or grass.
Eggs 4–8, white. 1 brood, sometimes 2.
Incubation 24–28 days
First flight 24–27 days
Food Small mammals, especially voles, and some small birds.

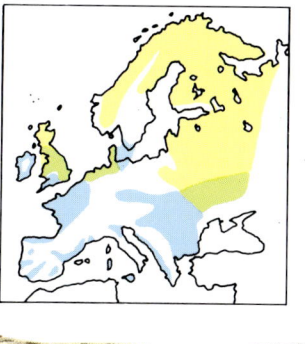

Short-eared owl

Cuckoo

CUCKOO
Cuculus canorus

Appearance Slim with long, pointed wings and a long tail. Has grey upper parts and head, and pale under-parts with barring.

Habits Flies with wings held down and rapid beats. Often holds wings down and raises tail when perching. Lays its eggs in the nests of other birds, such as the meadow pipit, dunnock, and reed warbler.
Status Summer visitor.
Size 33 cm (13 in)
Weight 105–130 g (3¾–4½ oz)
Song A far-carrying 'cu-coo', sometimes 'cu-cu-coo'.

Smaller dunnock feeding young cuckoo

Call The female has a chuckling call.
Nest Uses other birds' nests.
Eggs 6–18, colour depends on species chosen as foster-parents. Lays 1 egg in each nest.
Incubation 12 days. Pushes out other eggs or young on hatching.
First flight 20–23 days
Food Mainly insects, especially caterpillars.

OPEN COUNTRY AND UPLAND BIRDS

Skylark
Alauda arvensis

Appearance Streaky brown with a white-edged, long tail and pointed wings. The under-parts are white with dark streaks on the breast. It has a slight crest which can be raised.
Habits Sings endlessly in flight from high in the sky.

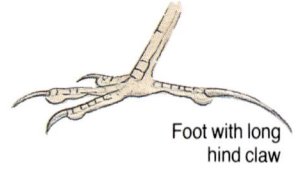

Foot with long hind claw

Walks or runs along the ground, sometimes crouching on bent legs.
Status Resident and winter visitor.
Size 18 cm (7 in)
Weight 35–45 g (1¼–1½ oz)
Song A loud, high warbling which can last several minutes, usually in flight.
Call Liquid 'chirrupp'.
Nest A cup of grass lined with fine grass and hair.
Nest site On the ground in clumps of grass.
Eggs 3–5, pale with brown speckles. 2 or 3 broods.
Incubation 11–12 days
First flight Leaves nest after 9–10 days and flies after 18–20 days.
Food Seeds, some worms, and insects.

Swallow

Skylark

Swallow
Hirundo rustica

Gaping beak

Appearance Slim with pointed wings and a forked tail with long streamers. It has blue-black upper parts, a chestnut throat, and cream under-parts.
Habits Spends a lot of time in the air. It is a graceful flier with a swooping, gliding flight. Skims the surface of water to drink and only lands on the ground to collect nest material. Forms large flocks in autumn.

Status Summer visitor.
Size 19 cm (7½ in)
Weight 16–25 g (about ¾ oz)
Song Twittering warble.
Call A high 'tswit, tswit, tswit'.
Nest Mud and straw.
Nest site Attached to a beam in a barn or shed.
Eggs 4–6, white with red spots. 2 broods.
Incubation 14–16 days
First flight 17–24 days
Food Insects caught in flight.

OPEN COUNTRY AND UPLAND BIRDS

MEADOW PIPIT
Anthus pratensis

Insect-eating beak

Appearance Slim with a green-brown back streaked with black. White underparts and buff breast with dark streaks.

Habits Spends most of its time on the ground, usually in small groups. Walks and runs, often wagging its tail. Likes heaths, moors, and dunes in summer, while during the winter it can be found on pastures, marshes, and coasts.
Status Resident and winter visitor.
Size 14 cm (5½ in)
Weight 16–25 g (about ¾ oz)
Song Usually sung in display flight, quiet then speeding up as the bird rises, ending with a trill as it 'parachutes' to the ground.
Call A high 'tsiip' often repeated 2 or 3 times.
Nest A cup of dry grass lined with finer grass and hair.
Nest site On the ground, hidden in a clump of grass or heather.
Eggs 4–5, white with grey-brown mottling. 2 broods.
Incubation 13–14 days
First flight 13–14 days
Food Insects, spiders, worms, and some seeds.

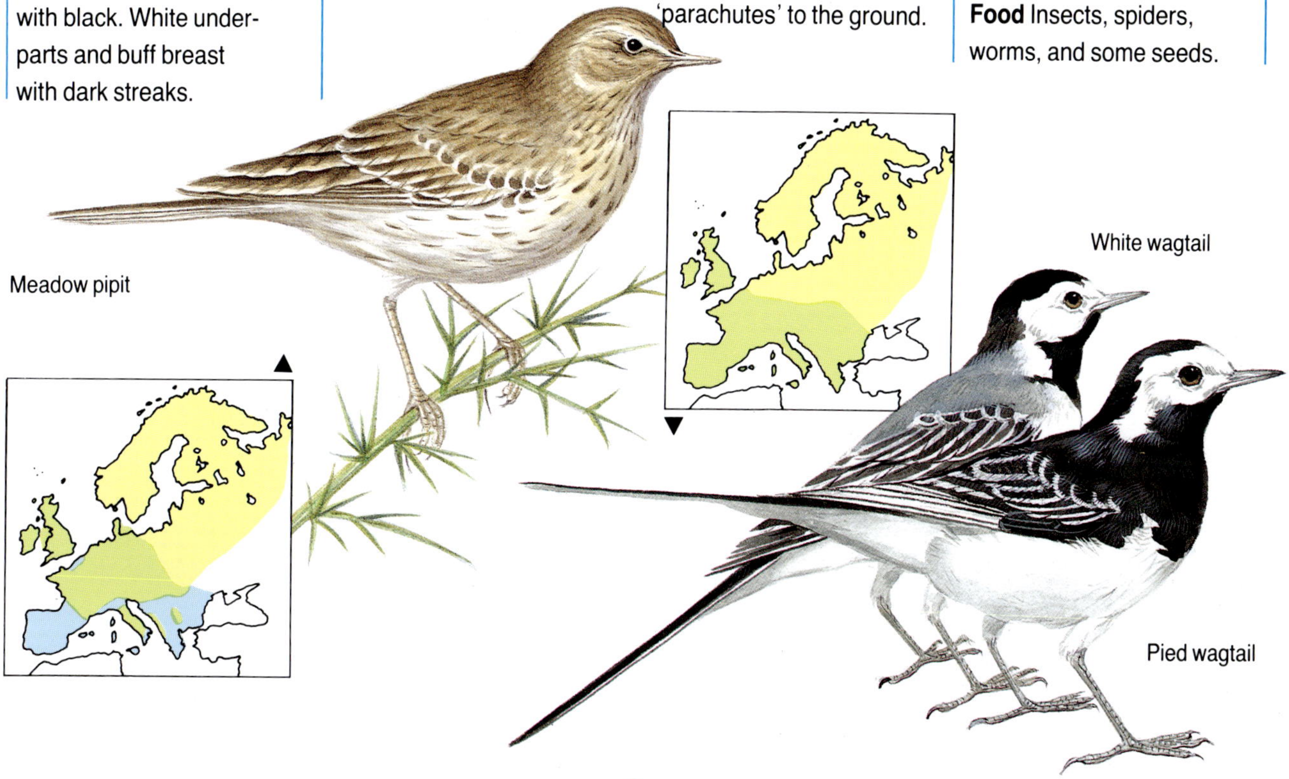

Meadow pipit

White wagtail

Pied wagtail

PIED WAGTAIL
Motacilla alba

Adult winter colouring

Appearance Slim with a long tail. Has black upper parts, throat, and upper breast with a white forehead, cheeks, and belly. The tail has white edges. In winter back is grey and throat is white. The white wagtail is the continental form and has a pale grey back.
Habits Usually found on open grass near water. Walks and runs with constant tail-wagging. Has a very bouncy flight. In autumn and winter it forms large roosts in reed-beds and often in trees in the middle of towns.
Status Resident and winter visitor. White wagtails are also summer visitors to parts of northern Europe.
Size 18 cm (7 in)
Weight 19–27 g (about ¾ oz)
Song A quiet, warbling twitter.
Call A sharp 'chissik'.
Nest A cup of grass, moss, and twigs lined with hair and feathers.
Nest site A hole in a bank or wall, or in a shed.
Eggs 5 or 6, pale grey with dark speckles. 2 broods.
Incubation 13–14 days
First flight 14–16 days
Food Mainly insects.

OPEN COUNTRY AND UPLAND BIRDS

REDWING
Turdus iliacus

Appearance A small thrush with a distinctive cream stripe above the eye and an orange-red side. Brown upper parts and white under-parts with dark spots. Orange-red underwing is visible in flight.
Habits Often found in grass fields with other thrushes, also in hawthorn hedges, feeding on berries. Migrates at night.
Status Winter visitor and rare breeder.
Size 21 cm (8½ in)
Weight 55–75 g (2–2½ oz)
Song A few fluty notes ending with a warble.
Call A thin 'seep' often given by migrating birds.
Nest A cup of grass and twigs lined with grass and moss.
Nest site In a tree or bush and sometimes on banks.
Eggs 5 or 6, blue-green with reddish spots. 2 broods.
Incubation 12–14 days
First flight 12–14 days
Food Worms, insects, and berries.

Orange-red underwing in flight

Redwing

FIELDFARE
Turdus pilaris

Appearance Large with a grey head, chestnut back, grey rump, and black tail. Has white under-parts, a yellow-brown breast with dark streaks and a yellow beak with black tip.
Habits Stands upright on the ground, often with wings drooping slightly. Runs or hops. Often noisy in flight. Found in open fields and in hedgerows, often with redwings.
Status Winter visitor and rare breeder.
Size 26 cm (10½ in)
Weight 80–140 g (2¾–5 oz)
Song A mixture of squeaks, chuckles, and fluty notes.
Call A loud 'chack, chack, chack' and a soft 'see'.
Nest A cup of grass and mud lined with fine grass.
Nest site Usually in a tree.
Eggs 4–6, blue with red-brown spots. 1 or 2 broods.
Incubation 13–14 days
First flight 12–14 days
Food Insects, worms, and berries.

Fieldfare

Yellow beak with black tip

OPEN COUNTRY AND UPLAND BIRDS

CARRION CROW
Corvus corone

Appearance All-black bird with a stout, black beak. The type known as the hooded crow has a grey back, breast, and belly. Distinguished from the rook by its black beak and lack of long thigh feathers.
Habits Tends not to form large flocks. Feeds mainly on the ground and flies slowly and deliberately.
Status Resident. Hooded crow resident and winter visitor, mainly found in northern and eastern Europe.
Size 47 cm (18¾ in)
Weight 540–600 g (19–21½ oz)
Call A deep 'kraah' that is sometimes repeated.
Nest A cup of twigs, earth, and moss lined with wool.
Nest sites Usually in a fork of a large tree.
Eggs 4–6, pale blue-green with darker spots. 1 brood.
Incubation 19 days
First flight 26–35 days
Food Grains, insects, small mammals, birds' eggs, and dead animals.

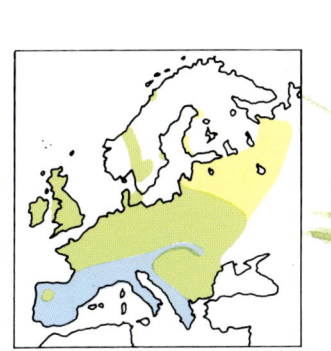

Calling position

ROOK
Corvus frugilegus

Appearance All black with a silvery-grey face and beak. Feathers around thighs tend to hang, giving a baggy appearance.
Habits Forms flocks more than the carrion crow and nests in a colony in a rookery. Feeds on the ground, usually in flocks. Roosts in large numbers, often with jackdaws (see page 37).

Calling position

Status Resident.
Size 46 cm (18½ in)
Weight 460–520 g (16½–18½ oz)
Call A loud 'taw' or 'kah'. Often noisy at the rookery.
Nest A large cup of sticks lined with grass and leaves.
Nest site Near the top of a tall tree with other nests in neighbouring trees.
Eggs 4–6, light blue-green with dark spots. 1 brood.
Incubation 16–19 days
First flight 29–30 days
Food Grains, roots, insects, and worms.

Carrion crow

Hooded crow

Rook

65

OPEN COUNTRY AND UPLAND BIRDS

MAGPIE
Pica pica

Appearance Large, black and white with a long tail. Its white shoulders and belly contrast with its black head, breast, back, and tail. The black feathers have a purple, green, and blue sheen.

Wing pattern in flight

Habits Perches in hedges or trees. Walks or hops on the ground. Often seen in groups.
Status Resident.
Size 46 cm (18½ in). The tail is 20–25 cm (8–10 in).
Weight 200–250 g (7–9 oz)
Call Harsh, chattering 'chakka-chakka-chak'.
Nest Domed and made of twigs with a lining of mud and roots.
Nest site In tall trees or hawthorn bushes.
Eggs 5–7, pale green with dark brown spots. 1 brood.
Incubation 17–18 days
First flight 22–27 days
Food Insects, seeds, berries, small mammals, and eggs.

Magpie

Goldfinch

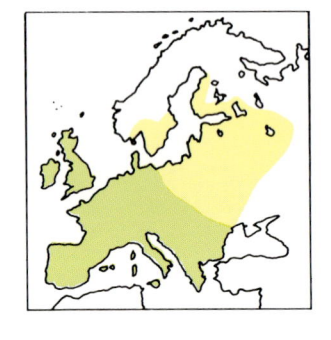

GOLDFINCH
Carduelis carduelis

Appearance Brightly coloured with a red face, white cheeks, and black crown. Has a golden-brown back and black wings with a bright yellow wing panel. Its belly is buff and white, tail black, and beak pale and pointed.

Pointed beak for eating small seeds

Habits Often found in noisy flocks, perching on thistle seed heads. It will hang upside down to get at seeds.
Status Resident.
Size 12 cm (4¾ in)
Weight 14–18 g (about ⅔ oz)
Song A fast, twittering and tinkling trill – 'witt-witt-wittoowit'.
Call A high, twittering 'tswitt-witt-witt'.
Nest A neat cup of grass, moss, and wool lined with hair and soft plant material.
Nest site In bushes and outer branches of trees.
Eggs 5–6, pale blue with brown spots and streaks. 2 broods.
Incubation 12–13 days
First flight 13–15 days
Food Seeds, especially thistle, and some insects.

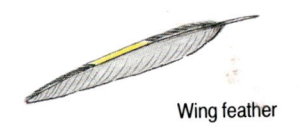

Wing feather

OPEN COUNTRY AND UPLAND BIRDS

LINNET
Carduelis cannabina

Appearance A streaky brown bird with a long forked tail. The male has a grey head, reddish-brown back, and red forehead and breast. The female has no red and is more streaked. Both have pale edges to the wings and tail.
Habits Gathers in flocks in autumn and winter. Perches on bushes and trees. Flies with slightly bouncy flight and hops when on the ground.

Sharp beak for eating seeds

Status Resident.
Size 13–14 cm (5–5½ in)
Weight 15–20 g (about ⅔ oz)
Song A musical twittering.
Call A chipping 'chichichichit' in flight, and also 'tsooeet'.
Nest A cup of grass and moss lined with hair and wool.
Nest site Bushes and hedges.
Eggs 4–6, pale blue with dark spots. 2 or 3 broods.
Incubation 12–13 days
First flight 11–13 days
Food Seeds and insects.

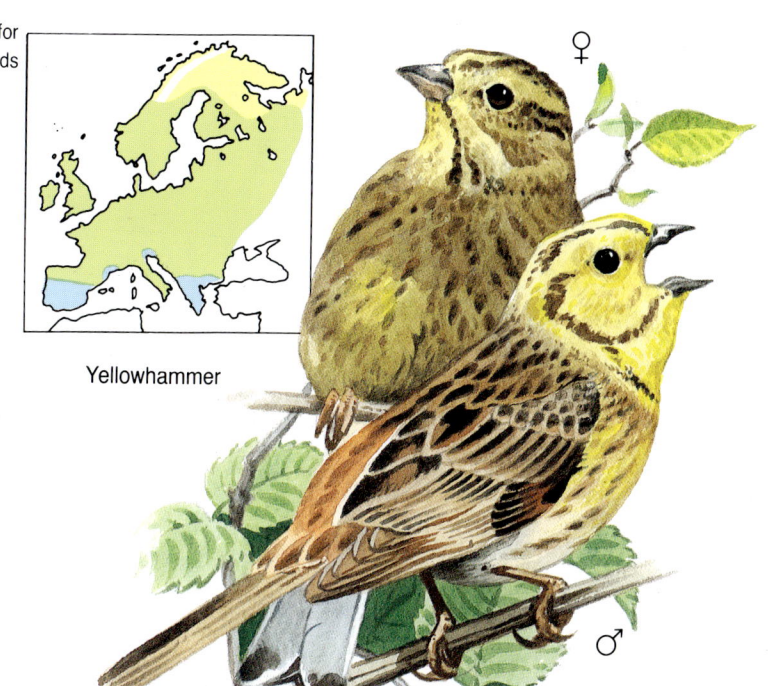

Yellowhammer

Linnet

YELLOW-HAMMER
Emberiza citrinella

Appearance Slim with a brown, streaked back and wings. The male has a bright yellow head and under-parts, and dark streaks on the side of the head and breast. The female is duller with less yellow. The tail has white edges and the rump is chestnut.

In flight showing white-edged tail and chestnut rump

Habits Often found in flocks in autumn and winter. Feeds on the ground, often with sparrows and finches. Sings from an open perch in a bush or hedge.
Status Resident.
Size 16.5 cm (6½ in)
Weight 24–30 g (about 1 oz)
Song A rapid series of notes ending with 'cheeeee' sounding like 'a little bit of bread and no cheese'.
Call A ringing 'tink'.
Nest A cup of grass lined with fine grass and hair.
Nest site Near the ground in a hedge or bush.
Eggs 3–5, whitish with dark spotting and scribbling. 2 or 3 broods.
Incubation 12–14 days
First flight 12–23 days
Food Seeds and insects.

River, Lake, and Marsh Birds

◄ Taking Note
These birdwatchers are well prepared. By carrying a rucksack, they have left their hands free to take notes. Wetlands like this are home to many birds, including the reed warbler, whose brown and white colouring means it is difficult to spot among the reeds. It is usually heard first.

You will find a variety of birds to watch near natural sources of water. This is because all birds need water to drink. Wetlands also attract birds because of the wide variety of food available there. Fish, frogs, snails, insects, and plants can all be easily found by any hungry bird.

It is not usually necessary to travel far to see wetland birds as some may be found in city parks. It can be very amusing simply to watch mallards when they 'up-end' themselves looking for food under the surface of a pond or lake.

However, many wetland areas are under threat. Marshes and wet meadows are being drained to turn into agricultural land or building areas. Rivers and lakes have become

RIVER, LAKE, AND MARSH BIRDS

polluted. So the best place to watch wetland birds is often in nature reserves and specially created gravel pits. Many reservoirs, too, have refuge areas where wildfowl can live undisturbed.

Birds that spend their time on the water have features that have become specially adapted for swimming over millions of years. Their feet especially have evolved to suit life in the water. They are sometimes used as paddles for swimming on the surface, but they also push diving birds along under the water (see box).

FEEDING FUN
It can be great fun to watch wetland birds feeding. Common terns and

▲ **Sitting Pretty**
Male tufted ducks like this are easily identified by their drooping crest. Using their webbed feet, tufted ducks will dive from the surface of the water to a depth of 2m (6 ft) in search of food. They like to eat water plants, as well as insects, frogs, and small fish. Tufted ducks often form colonies.

DESIGNER FEET
Different water birds have evolved different types of feet to suit their needs. Grebes and coots both have flaps of skin along each toe that help them to swim. Ducks, geese, swans, and gulls have a flap between each toe. These flaps open out to push back against the water like a paddle, and close flat when bringing the feet forward.

Grebe

Duck

Coot

RIVER, LAKE, AND MARSH BIRDS

UNDERWATER FOOD

Much of the food eaten by waterbirds is hidden under water. If you are lucky, you may see a bird surfacing with fish or insects in its beak.

▲ Dragonfly larvae are food for grebes and herons.

▲ Water lice are eaten by kingfishers and dippers.

▲ Midge larvae are a favourite of many water birds.

▲ Water boatmen live close to the surface. Ducks and grebes love them.

▲ Great pond snails form a large part of the tufted duck's winter diet.

kingfishers put on a great display. They dive from the air into the water to catch fish. The tern does this in flight, hovering over the water before diving. The kingfisher dives off a perch. You will probably just see it as a flash of blue speeding down a river or across a gravel pit.

Grey herons have long legs and long necks. This lets them wade into deep water and reach out quickly to snatch a fish or frog. Mute swans stretch out their long necks to reach under the water to feed on a variety of water plants.

Some wetland birds, such as warblers, wagtails, swallows, and martins, survive on insects. Look out for the brightly coloured yellow wagtail that thrives on all the insects in marshes or wet meadows. It often feeds near cattle, flying after the insects that the animals disturb as they walk along. Insect-eating birds

◀ **Pond Dipping**
You can use a fine-meshed net to fish all sorts of creatures out of ponds. Diving beetles, tadpoles, dragonfly nymphs, whirligig beetles, pond skaters, and water boatmen will all be gobbled up by birds. Even frogs may be eaten by herons.

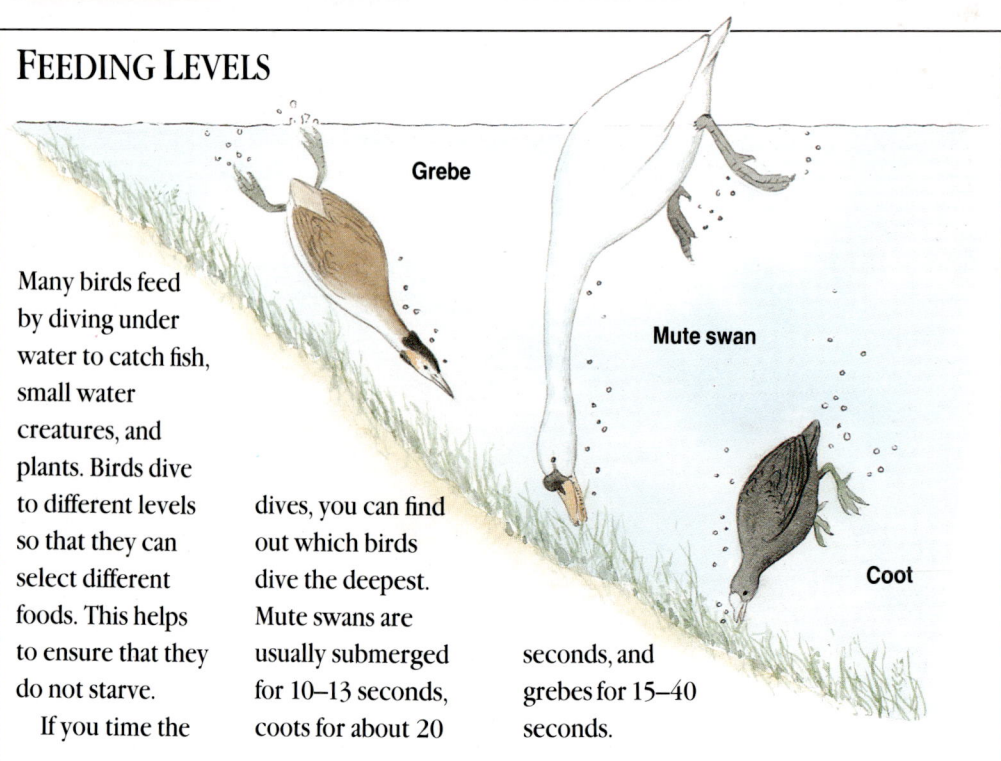

FEEDING LEVELS

Many birds feed by diving under water to catch fish, small water creatures, and plants. Birds dive to different levels so that they can select different foods. This helps to ensure that they do not starve.

If you time the dives, you can find out which birds dive the deepest. Mute swans are usually submerged for 10–13 seconds, coots for about 20 seconds, and grebes for 15–40 seconds.

70

RIVER, LAKE, AND MARSH BIRDS

migrate south in the winter when their food source disappears.

The water birds that remain through the winter, such as kingfishers and herons, have difficulty finding food when lakes and rivers freeze. If you are near the coast you may see them looking for unfrozen water there. But many still die of starvation.

THE WATER'S EDGE

Along the water's edge you will be able to watch birds like coots, moorhens, and great-crested grebes. They build their nests in the bankside plants or on floating mats of weeds.

The best place to find reed warblers is – as their name suggests – in reeds and rushes at the edge of the water. Their loud songs give them away. If you are patient and quiet, you may be able to watch them climb up a stem and sing from the top. Sedge warblers, however, like thicker vegetation. They are usually found singing in a bush or brambles.

WATERSIDE NESTS

Grebes, coots, and moorhens make their nests of grass and weed, hiding them in reeds surrounded by water. The female mute swan uses sticks and reeds that the male collects to build a huge nest at the water's edge. Grey herons, which spend their time feeding by water, build large nests made of sticks very high in the trees. Some small birds, such as house sparrows, build their nests in the side of the heron's nest.

▶ **Bright Blue**
The kingfisher's clear blue and green upper parts and chestnut under-parts make it one of the most colourful birds. It looks like a blue flash as it darts over the water.

▲ **Private Lives**
Sedge warblers are often hidden among thick waterside plants. But watch carefully and you may see one perching out in the open. Listen out too for its song of both harsh and sweet notes.

▲ **Gone Fishing**
The grey heron's long neck and sharply pointed beak are used for spearing fish and tearing apart the flesh.

RIVER, LAKE, AND MARSH BIRDS

GREAT CRESTED GREBE
Podiceps cristatus

Appearance Its long upright neck and long beak are visible when it sits on the water. Long brown feathers form a frill around its face in breeding plumage. In winter its face and cheeks are white.

Lobes on toes

Habits Feeds by diving from the surface of lakes and reservoirs. Rarely flies, and dives when disturbed. Usually seen singly or in pairs and sometimes in small groups in winter.
Status Resident.
Size 48 cm (19¼ in)
Weight 750–1200 g (1⅔–2⅔ lb)

Call A loud 'jik, jik, jik' and a barking 'gorrr'.
Nest A heap of floating vegetation.
Nest site Among reeds close to the water's edge.
Eggs 3 or 4, white, becoming dirty.
1 or 2 broods.
Incubation 28 days
First flight Swims at once and becomes independent after 10 weeks.
Food Fish, some insects, and snails.

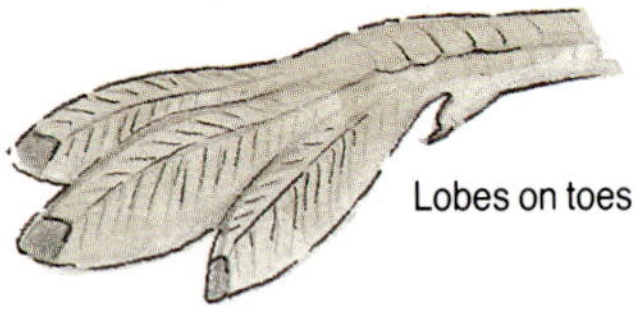

Great crested grebe

Grey heron

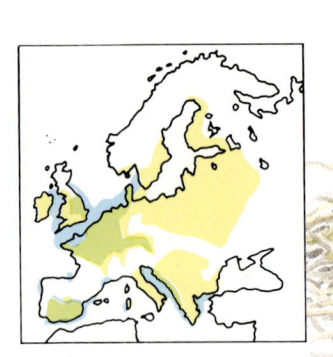

GREY HERON
Ardea cinerea

Appearance Tall, grey and white with long legs and a long neck. Wings are long and broad, and the neck is pulled back in flight.

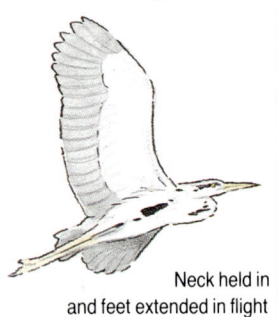

Neck held in and feet extended in flight

Habits Walks slowly and often stands extremely still when feeding, holding its neck curved ready to snatch a fish.
Status Resident.
Size 90 cm (36 in). The body is about 40 cm (16 in).
Weight 1600–2000 g (3½–4½ lb)
Call A loud, harsh 'fraank'.
Nest Built of branches and sticks lined with twigs.
Nest site In high trees where large colonies can be established.
Eggs 3–5, blue.
1 or 2 broods.
Incubation 25 days
First flight 50–55 days
Food Fish, water voles, and frogs.

CANADA GOOSE
Branta canadensis

Canada goose

Appearance A large and long-necked goose with grey-brown body, black neck, and white cheek and throat patch.

Flock in flight

Habits Forms large flocks which often migrate in 'V' formation but forms looser groups for short flights.
Status Resident, introduced to Britain and parts of northern Europe.
Size 95 cm (38 in)
Weight 2900–4000 g (6½–9 lb)
Call A loud honking 'wah-onk'.
Nest Lined with grass and down feathers.
Nest site On the ground in a hollow on an island or in marshy vegetation.
Eggs 5 or 6, cream. 1 brood.
Incubation 28–30 days
First flight Mobile immediately and flies after 6–7 weeks.
Food Grass, water plants, and grain.

MUTE SWAN
Cygnus olor

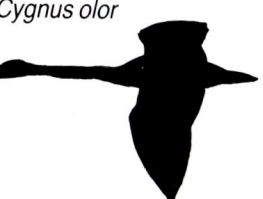

Appearance A large, white water bird with a curved neck and orange beak. The male has a large black knob above its beak. The young are grey.

Broad beak for pulling at weeds

Habits Found on lakes, gravel pits, and slow-moving rivers. Walks very awkwardly, and in flight its wings make a low whistling sound. Aggressive towards other swans. Feeds by dipping its neck under water.

Feeding with neck under water

Status Resident.

Size 150–160 cm (60–64 in)
Weight 10,000–12,000 g (22–27 lb)
Call Usually silent but grunts and hisses occasionally.
Nest A large mound of reeds and water weeds.
Nest site On the ground near water.
Eggs 5–8, green-white. 1 brood.
Incubation 35 days
First flight Swims soon after hatching and flies after 4–5 months.
Food Water weeds and grass.

Mute swan

73

RIVER, LAKE, AND MARSH BIRDS

Mallard
Anas platyrhynchos

Appearance The male has a grey-brown body, a dark brown breast, a green head with a yellow beak, and orange legs. The female is mottled brown. Both show a purple-blue wing patch that is edged with white in flight.

Wing in flight

Habits Flies fast with shallow wing-beats. Feeds on the surface of water, up-ending but not diving.
Status Resident.
Size 58 cm (23 in)
Weight 850–1400 g (2–3 lb)
Call A loud, quacking 'kwark kwark' and a quieter 'rait'.
Nest Lined with leaves, grass, and down.
Nest site Hidden among plants on the ground and sometimes in tree holes.
Eggs 9–13, green-buff. 1 brood.
Incubation 28 days
First flight Swims almost immediately and flies after 7–8 weeks.
Food Seeds, plants, insects, and worms.

Mallard

Tufted Duck
Aythya fuligula

Appearance The eyes are yellow and the beak grey with a black tip. The male is black with white sides and a long, drooping crest. The female is dark brown with a short crest.

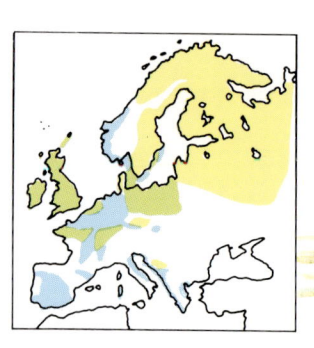

Beak with black tip

Habits Dives for food from the surface of the water and often moves to deeper water if disturbed. Flies with rapid wing-beats.
Status Resident and winter visitor.
Size 43 cm (17 in)
Weight 550–900 g (1¼ oz–2 lb)
Call A growling 'krrr, krrr' made by the female.
Nest Lined with grass and down feathers.
Nest site In thick grass or rushes near water.

Tufted duck

Eggs 8–11, green-grey. 1 brood.
Incubation 25 days
First flight Swims and dives immediately and flies after 45–50 days.
Food Insects, snails, frogs, small fish, and some vegetation.

Male's white wing bar

RIVER, LAKE, AND MARSH BIRDS

MOORHEN
Gallinula chloropus

Appearance A dumpy black water bird with grey under-parts. It has a white undertail and white stripe along each side. The beak is red with a yellow tip. Its long green legs have long toes.

Habits The head moves back and forth as the bird swims and its tail is often held cocked. Flies low and weakly with legs dangling. Will feed in grass fields some distance from water.

Status Resident.

Position of legs in flight

Foot with long toes

Size 35 cm (14 in)
Weight 250–420 g (9–15 oz)
Call A croaking 'curruk' and a high 'kik'.
Nest Dead reeds and grasses.
Nest site Hidden in thick bank-side vegetation.
Eggs 5–9, pale brown with darker blotches. 2 or 3 broods.
Incubation 21–22 days
First flight Leaves nest after a few days and flies after 6–7 weeks.
Food Seeds, grass, leaves, insects, and worms.

Moorhen

Coot

COOT
Fulica atra

Appearance A stout, all black water bird with a white beak and forehead. It has grey-green legs with long, lobed toes.

Frontal shield on beak

Habits Found in large flocks, especially in winter. Patters along the water before taking off. Dives for food from the surface of the water.
Status Resident and winter visitor.
Size 38 cm (15 in)
Weight 650–900 g (1½–2 lb)
Call A squawking 'kowk' and a higher 'tewk'.
Nest Large, built up from dead reeds.
Nest site Among reeds or other thick water plants.
Eggs 6–9, light brown with darker spots. 1 brood, sometimes 2.
Incubation 21–24 days
First flight Fed by parents for 1 month, then gains independence after 55–60 days.
Food Water plants, grass, seeds, insects, and snails.

RIVER, LAKE, AND MARSH BIRDS

BLACK-HEADED GULL
Larus ridibundus

Appearance A grey and white bird with black wing-tips, red legs and a slender, dark red beak. It has a dark brown hood in summer and black cheek spot in winter.
Habits Common on inland fields, gravel pits, and reservoirs, as well as coastal marshes and estuaries. Often found in flocks. Feeds in shallow water, mud, and ploughed fields by catching insects in the air.
Status Resident and winter visitor.
Size 36 cm (14½ in)
Weight 225–350 g (8–12½ oz)
Call A harsh 'kwaa' and short 'kuk'.
Nest Plant material.
Nest site In colonies on the ground in clumps of grass.
Eggs 3, green-brown with dark blotches. 1 brood.
Incubation 23–26 days
First flight 5–6 weeks
Food Insects, snails, worms, and seeds.

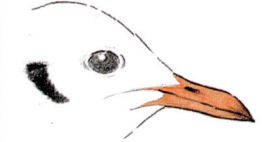

Winter colouring

COMMON TERN
Sterna hirundo

Appearance A slim, grey and white bird with a black cap, black-tipped red beak, and short, red legs. Has long, pointed wings and a long, narrow, forked tail.

Black-tipped red beak

Habits Flies gracefully, hovering or flying slowly before diving from the air into water for food.
Status Summer visitor.
Size 35 cm (14 in)
Weight 90–150 g (3–5⅓ oz)
Call A high, grating 'keee-ah'. Also 'kik-kik-kik' and 'kirri-kirri'.
Nest Simple hollow.
Nest site On the ground on shingle or sand, often among grasses.
Eggs 2 or 3, creamy-brown. 1 brood.
Incubation 22–26 days
First flight 21–26 days
Food Mainly fish and some worms and snails.

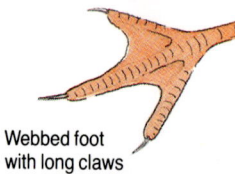

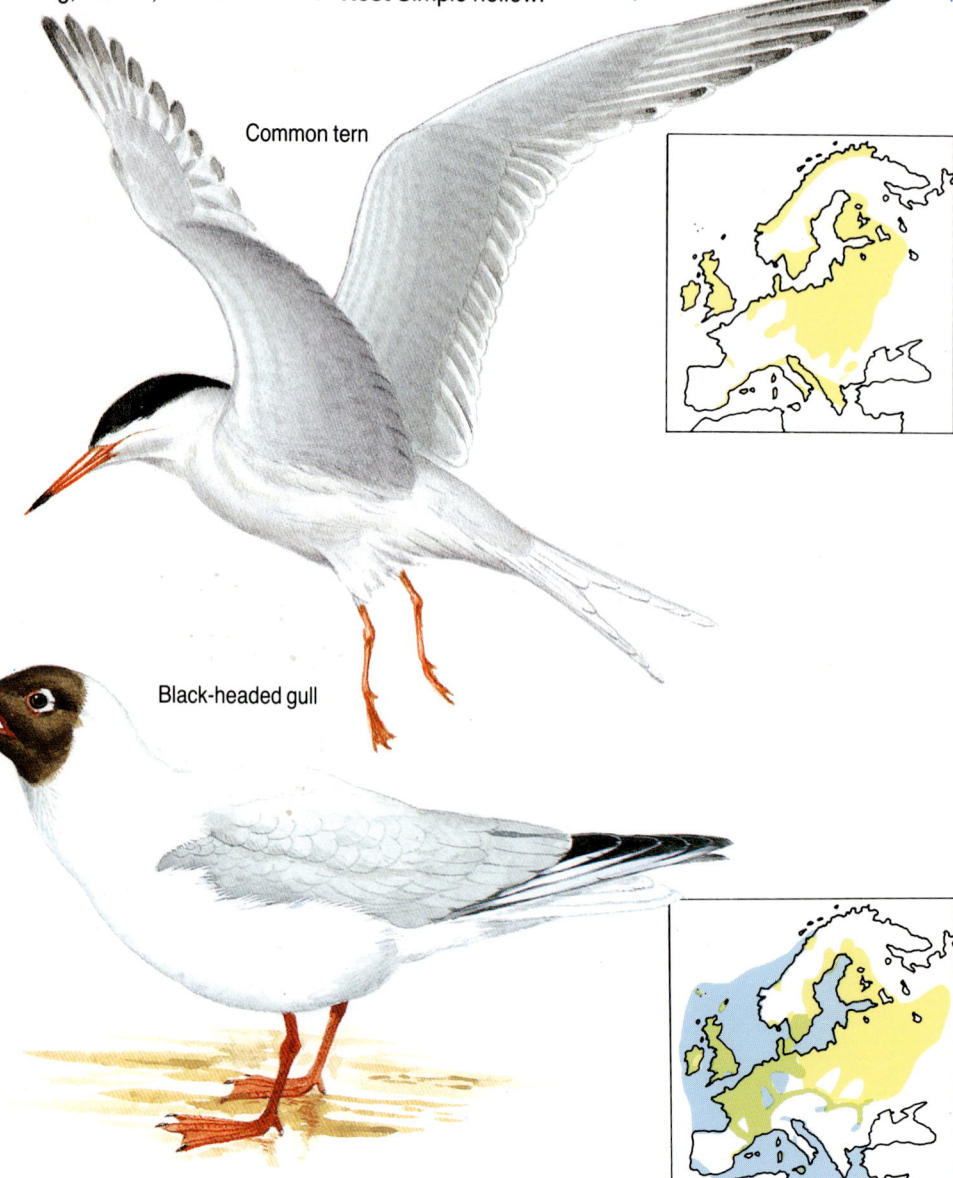

Webbed foot with long claws

Common tern

Black-headed gull

RIVER, LAKE, AND MARSH BIRDS

KINGFISHER
Alcedo atthis

Kingfisher

Appearance Dumpy and tail-less with green-blue upper parts and chestnut under-parts. Has a white throat and cheek patch, and a long dagger-like beak. Foot has toes of different lengths and 2 toes partly joined.

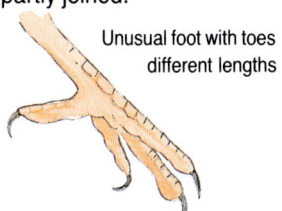

Unusual foot with toes different lengths

Habits Found along rivers, gravel pits, and lakes. Often seen only as a flash of blue flying low over the water. Dives into the water from a perch or hovers over the surface.
Status Resident.
Size 16 cm (6½ in)
Weight 40–45 g (1½ oz)
Call A shrill 'chee' often repeated.
Nest No material used.
Nest site A chamber at the end of a burrow in an earth bank.
Eggs 5–7, white. 2 broods.
Incubation 19–21 days
First flight 23–27 days
Food Small fish.

DIPPER
Cinclus cinclus

Appearance Plump, short-tailed, and black with a brown head. Has a white throat and breast.
Habits Likes fast-flowing rivers. When perched on a rock it bobs up and down. Flies low and fast. Feeds by walking or plunging into water. It can walk under water.
Status Resident.
Size 18 cm (7 in)
Weight 55–75 g (2–2½ oz)
Song A clear warbling.
Call A loud 'zit, zit, zit' or sharp 'clink'.
Nest Roofed, with moss and dry grass and lined with leaves.
Nest site In a hole in banks, walls, and bridges next to water.
Eggs 4–6, white. 2 broods.
Incubation 16 days
First flight 19–25 days
Food Water insects, snails, and worms.

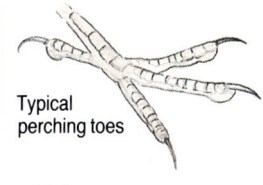

Typical perching toes

Dipper

RIVER, LAKE, AND MARSH BIRDS

SEDGE WARBLER
Acrocephalus schoenobaenus

Appearance Small and brown with a streaked back and white under-parts. Has a broad cream stripe above the eye. Young are pale coloured around crown.

Habits Likes thick vegetation and hedges near water. Frequently keeps to thick cover but it can also be seen perching openly on bushes and tall plants.
Status Summer visitor.
Size 13 cm (5 in)
Weight 10–13 g (about 2/5 oz)
Song A chattering warble with some musical phrases, often given in song flight.
Call A loud 'tut' and a churring note.
Nest A deep cup of grass, moss, and spiders' webs lined with hair, grass heads, or feathers.
Nest site Above the ground in vegetation or in a bush.
Eggs 5 or 6, pale with darker blotches and marks. 1 or 2 broods.
Incubation 13–14 days
First flight 12–14 days
Food Insects and spiders. Eats berries in autumn.

Young bird's pale colouring along crown

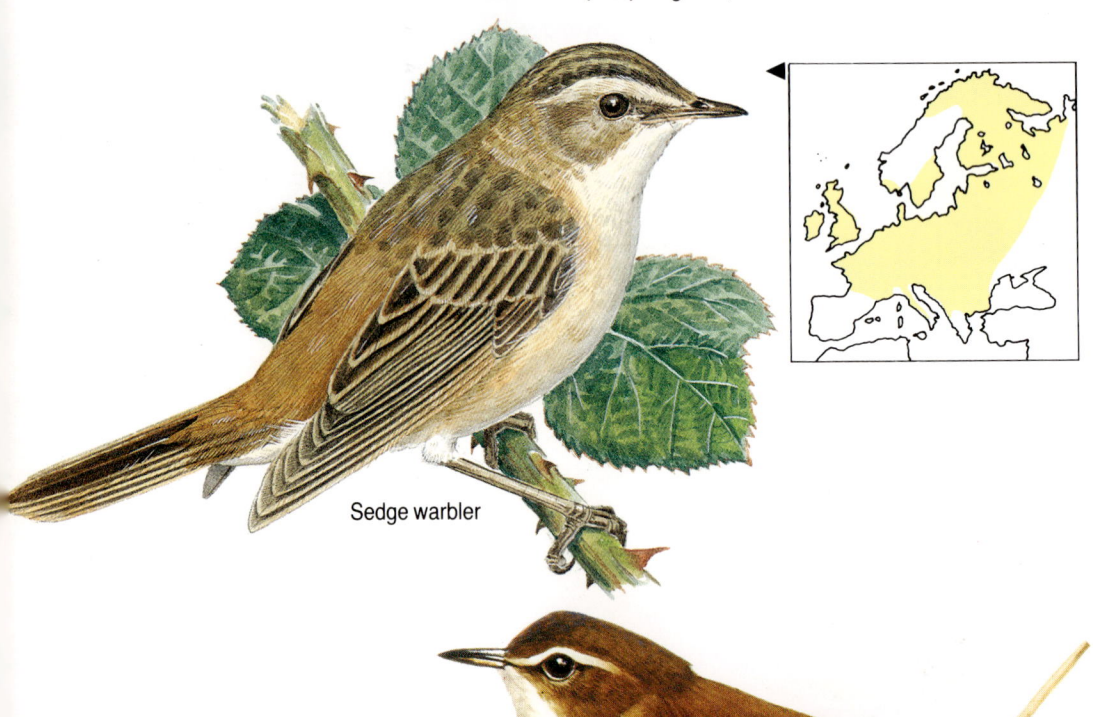

Sedge warbler

REED WARBLER
Acrocephalus scirpaceus

Appearance Slim, unstreaked brown with white under-parts and a faint, narrow, pale strip above the eye. The beak is fairly long.

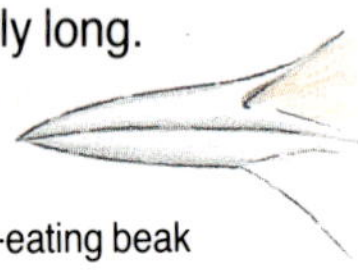

Insect-eating beak

Habits Found mainly in reed-beds and vegetation next to water. It clings to stems, often remaining hidden.
Status Summer visitor.
Size 13 cm (5 in)
Weight 10–15 g (about 2/5 oz)
Song A loud warbling with phrases often repeated 2 or 3 times – 'jag, jag, jag . . . krr, krr, krr . . .'.
Call Chacking and churring notes.
Nest A deep cup of grasses and reed flowers lined with wool, hair, and fine grass. It is built around reed stems.
Nest sites Reed beds.
Eggs 3–5, white with green or grey blotches. 2 broods.
Incubation 11–12 days
First flight 11–12 days
Food Insects, spiders, and slugs. Eats berries in autumn.

Reed warbler

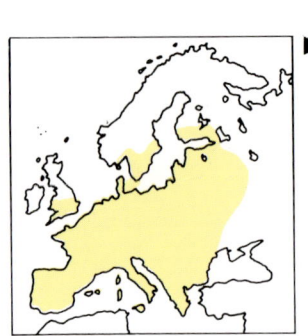

RIVER, LAKE, AND MARSH BIRDS

REED BUNTING
Emberiza schoeniclus

Appearance The back is brown with darker streaks and the under-parts are white. The male has a black head and a throat with a white collar in summer. The female has a brown head with a pale eye-stripe and a throat with a dark 'moustache' stripe. The tail has white sides.
Habits Creeps or hops on the ground and perches on tall vegetation or clings to stems. Likes damp areas but often found well away from water. Sometimes visits gardens in winter.
Status Resident.

Insect-eating beak – shorter than reed warbler's

Size 15 cm (6 in)
Weight 15–22 g (about ⅔ oz)
Song A slow 'jip, jip, jip, tiu, tittik'.
Call A shrill 'tseeu' and a ringing 'chink'.
Nest A cup of grass and moss lined with fine grass and hair.
Nest site On or near the ground in clumps of grass and bushes.
Eggs 4 or 5, buff with darker streaks. 2 broods.
Incubation 13–14 days
First flight 10–13 days
Food Small seeds and insects.

Reed bunting

YELLOW WAGTAIL
Motacilla flava

Appearance Slim with a long, white-edged tail. The male has greenish upper parts and bright yellow under-parts. The female is paler, and the young are brown with a dark throat marking.
Habits Feeds in wet meadows and by gravel pits and rivers. It is often found in groups, walking or running alongside cows and other large animals wagging its tail.
Status Summer visitor.
Size 17 cm (7 in)
Weight 16–22 g (about ⅔ oz)
Song A short warbling which includes call notes.
Call A loud 'tsweeep'.
Nest A cup of grass stems and roots lined with hair.
Nest site On the ground in thick grass.
Eggs 5 or 6, pale with darker speckles. 2 broods.
Incubation 12–13 days
First flight 12–13 days
Food Mainly insects.

Yellow wagtail

Young bird's head

Coast and Estuary Birds

WARNING!

As sea coasts can be dangerous, here are some rules to follow:
- Never go alone and always let someone know where you are.
- Check when the tide comes in and leave in good time.
- Wear sturdy shoes with a good grip. Wet rocks are slippery.
- Do not go near the shore if you cannot swim.
- Wear warm, waterproof clothes. Coastal areas are colder than inland.

Coastlines provide a home for many different species of bird and so are ideal places to birdwatch. A variety of seabirds breed on cliffs and islands. You can watch waders along sandy or shingle beaches, or look out for many types of wildfowl along salt-marshes and estuaries. (An estuary is the wide mouth of a river.)

THROUGH THE YEAR

Hundreds of thousands of seabirds migrate to the coast each spring to breed. They nest on sea cliffs that predators cannot reach.

A seabird colony in summer is a place of frantic activity. Kittiwakes scream and wheel around cliff faces. Herring gulls squabble over food scraps. Puffins fly out to sea and back to bring food to their young. Cormorants dive deep under water in their search for fish to feed on.

SEA FOOD

Food for birds is normally plentiful around coasts, but overfishing by people can cause shortages. Cormorants and puffins dive under water to catch fish, while kittiwakes pick their food from the surface of the sea.

▲ Sand eels are food for puffins, cormorants, and kittiwakes.

▲ Herring gulls and kittiwakes eat mussels.

▲ Most sea birds will eat cod.

▲ Cormorants love to feed on crabs.

In the winter, many of these birds spend all their time out at sea, where they both feed and sleep. Sometimes bad weather forces them to the shore, but usually they only come back on land in spring to breed.

WHAT TO WATCH

Estuaries are important as feeding and roosting areas for waders and for wildfowl, such as wigeons and shelducks. Many migrant birds also stop off at estuaries to feed and rest before continuing journeys to their breeding areas in northern Europe or wintering grounds in West Africa.

A good place to watch dunlins, curlews, redshanks, and other waders is on mud uncovered by falling tides. Worms, shrimps, and

▲ **Noisy Eaters**
Large, noisy flocks of gulls can often be observed flying over harbours and fishing fleets. They are looking for the remains of the day's catch to eat. In the winter, gulls fly even further inland looking for food. Herring gulls, a common resident and winter visitor, eat shellfish, the remains of fish and small animals, and even rubbish from inland dumps.

COAST AND ESTUARY BIRDS

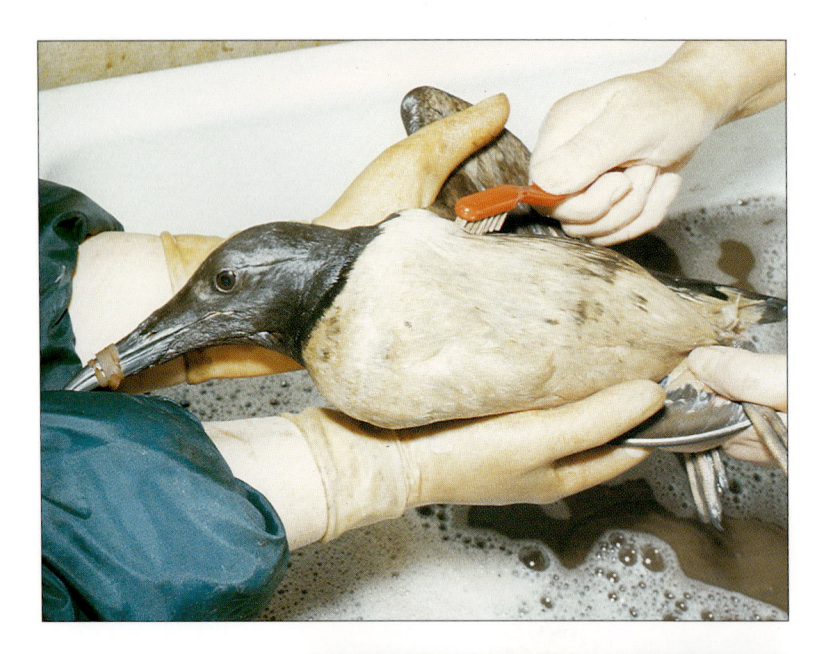

OIL HAZARD

Oil spills can result from accidents when tankers run aground or break up at sea. The pollution they cause can damage coastal habitats and kill birds.

Oil floats on water and will spread out to form a thin layer, called a slick. If oil gets onto a bird's feathers it destroys the natural waterproofing, the feathers become waterlogged, and the bird can drown or starve. Oiled birds should only be cleaned by experts (above).

▲ **Spot the Eggs**
These ringed plover eggs look like stones, so are not visible to predators.

▼ **Wading Curlew**
Curlews can stride through quite deep water because of their long feet.

snails live under the surface. Only the long beaks of waders can probe down deep enough to find these animals. Curlews can reach down the furthest into the mud because of their very long beaks. Small waders, like dunlins, pick up the tinier snails with their shorter beaks.

When tides are high you will see waders roosting on the shore, in salt-marshes, or in fields. Large flocks of waders can be seen around the coast in winter moving from feeding to roosting places. Some waders have particular feeding places on the coast. Sanderlings, for example, are nearly always found on sandy beaches at the edge of the water.

Ringed plovers and oyster-catchers like to breed on pebbly beaches. Their eggs blend in well with the stones and are almost invisible. If the ringed plover is disturbed from its nest it will pretend to have broken a wing. This 'trick' leads an intruder, such as a fox, away from the eggs or the chicks.

The sea itself can be a good place to look for birds because it provides food for them. Terns dive spectacularly from the air, plunging into the water and surfacing with

PROBING BEAKS

Water birds' beaks have evolved to suit their diets, and the great variety of beak lengths ensures that each species of bird reaches different foods below the surface of the water.

COAST AND ESTUARY BIRDS

fresh fish in their beaks. You can also watch puffins and cormorants sit on the surface, then dive down to swim in pursuit of their food.

STAYING ALIVE

Coastal areas can also be very important for the survival of birds during especially cold winters. When temperatures fall below freezing inland, the coast is usually slightly warmer and currents help keep sea water unfrozen. Waders, like redshanks, and water birds, such as herons and kingfishers, often fly to the coast to feed when their inland habitats freeze.

▲ **Puffins on Parade**
A brightly-coloured triangular beak makes the puffin easy to recognize. The blue-grey, red, and gold stripes are most colourful in summer when puffins are on land for breeding. The colours become duller when the birds live on water.

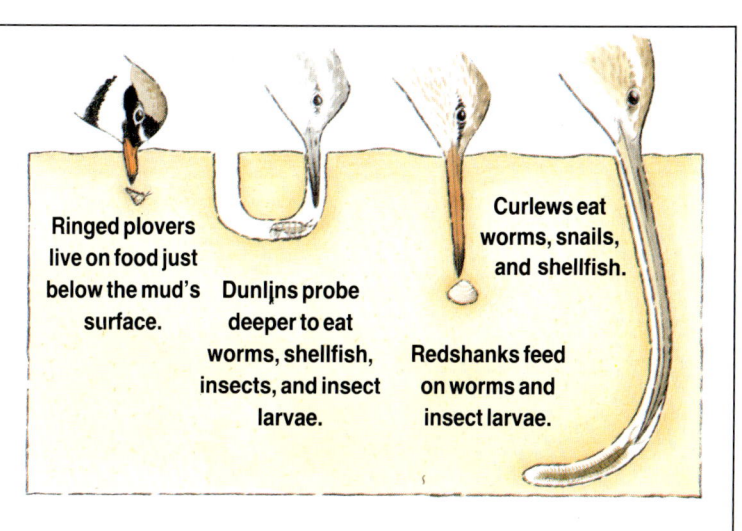

Ringed plovers live on food just below the mud's surface.

Dunlins probe deeper to eat worms, shellfish, insects, and insect larvae.

Curlews eat worms, snails, and shellfish.

Redshanks feed on worms and insect larvae.

SEABIRD CITY

Different seabirds have their own nesting places in a seabird colony. Even though thousands of birds will be flying around frantically, each bird can find its own small piece of cliff and protect it. The ledges will be used by kittiwakes which often have only just enough room for themselves and their chicks. Puffins usually breed on the grassy tops of a cliff, in burrows or crevices in the rocks. Cormorants prefer to breed on rocky areas close to the bottom of the cliff. Herring gulls will nest on grassy outcrops near to the top, but can also be found on suitable ledges near the bottom. Apart from occasional squabbling over food and space, these birds live happily side by side – a real seabird city.

Herring gulls

Puffins

Kittiwakes

Cormorants

COAST AND ESTUARY BIRDS

CORMORANT
Phalacrocorax carbo

Appearance A large, black, and long-necked bird with a short tail and a long beak. Adults have a white throat and white thigh patches.

Long, hooked beak

Habits Found around coasts and on inland water in winter. Sits on rocks and dives for food from the surface of the water. Often stands on a rock with its wings outstretched.

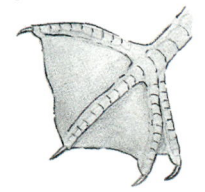

Foot with 4 webbed toes

Status Resident.
Size 90 cm (36 in)
Weight 2000–2500 g (4½–5½ lb)
Call A croaking noise made when at the nest.
Nest A loose construction of seaweed or sticks.
Nest site On cliff ledges and sometimes in trees.
Eggs 3 or 4, pale blue. 1 brood.
Incubation 28–31 days
First flight 50 days
Food Fish.

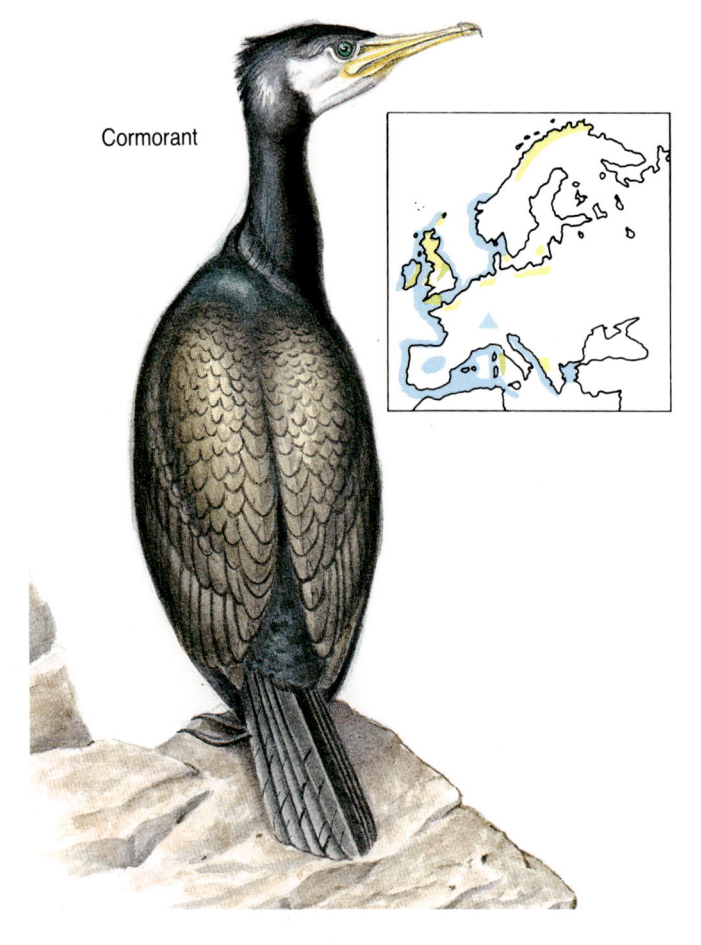

Cormorant

Puffin

PUFFIN
Fratercula arctica

Appearance Black and white with a round, white cheek patch and a brightly coloured triangular beak. The upper parts are black and the under-parts are white.

Winter beak colouring

Habits Feeds by diving from the surface of the water. Flies with rapid wing-beats. Often sits in groups on the sea.
Status Summer visitor, sometimes seen offshore at other times.
Size 30 cm (12 in)
Weight 400–500 g (14–18 oz)
Call A growling noise made when it is in its burrow.
Nest Bits of plant material.
Nest site In a burrow in a grassy slope or crevice in rocks.
Eggs 1, white. 1 brood.
Incubation 39–43 days
First flight 38–44 days
Food Fish and shrimp.

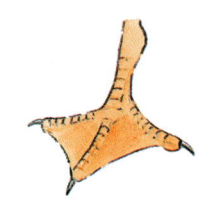

Foot with 3 webbed toes

COAST AND ESTUARY BIRDS

KITTIWAKE
Rissa tridactyla

Appearance A grey and white gull with distinctive 'dipped-in-ink' black wing-tips. Young birds have dark markings which form a 'W' across the wings.
Habits Found in very noisy colonies. Often sits on the sea in groups.
Status Summer visitor to breeding colonies, found offshore at other times. Sometimes blown inland during gales.
Size 41 cm (16½ in)
Weight 300–500 g (11–18 oz)
Call Loud 'kittiwaak'
Nest Seaweed and mud.
Nest site On cliff ledges and occasionally on buildings by the coast.
Eggs 2 or 3, grey or brown. 1 brood.
Incubation 25–32 days
First flight 33–54 days
Food Small fish and shrimp.

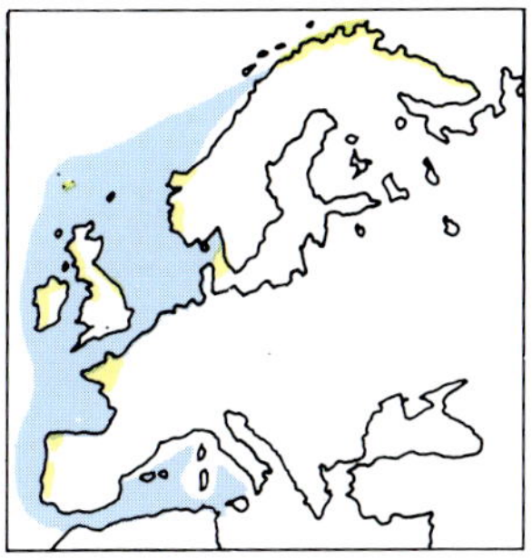

Black wing-tips

Kittiwake

HERRING GULL
Larus argentatus

Appearance A large, grey and white gull. The wing-tips are black with white spots. Young birds are dark brown and take 4 years to reach adult plumage.

Distinctive red spot on adult beak

Habits Spends the breeding season on the coasts and comes inland for winter. Noisy and aggressive, it sometimes chases smaller seabirds to make them drop food.
Status Resident.
Size 60 cm (24 in)
Weight 750–1250 g (1⅔–2¾ lb)
Call A ringing 'kee-ow' that is repeated.
Nest Grass and seaweed.
Nest site On cliff ledges and sometimes on roofs.
Eggs 3, olive-brown. 1 brood.
Incubation 28–30 days
First flight 35–40 days
Food Fish, dead animals, and scraps.

Webbed foot with hind toe

Herring gull

85

COAST AND ESTUARY BIRDS

WIGEON
Anas penelope

Appearance The male has a chestnut head with an orange crown, grey body, and black tail and under-tail coverts. A white patch at the front of the wing can be seen clearly in flight. The female shows a pale belly in flight. A rounded head helps to identify females.

Fine feather markings

Short beak used for grazing

Habits Feeds by grazing and is often found in large flocks on salt-marshes, grassy edges of reservoirs, and gravel pits.
Status Resident, passage migrant, and winter visitor.
Size 46 cm (18½ in)
Weight 700–900 g (1½–2 lb)
Call A clear whistling note – 'wee-oo'.
Nest Grass lined with down feathers.
Nest site On the ground in grass, heather, or bracken.
Eggs 7–9, cream coloured. 1 brood.
Incubation 24–25 days
First flight 40–45 days
Food Leaves and roots.

Wigeon

Shelduck

SHELDUCK
Tadorna tadorna

Appearance A large and goose-like duck. Its body is mainly white with a glossy green head and a chestnut breast band. Has a large red beak and pink legs. The male has a red knob at the base of its beak.

Male beak

Habits Flies with slow wing-beats and swims less than other ducks. Usually seen in groups and large flocks. Young from several parents often looked after by 1 or 2 females in a 'crèche'.
Status Resident.
Size 60 cm (24 in)
Weight 1100–1450 g (2½–3⅓ lb)
Call Males give a high whistle and females give a 'ak-ak-ak'.
Nest Pale grey down feathers and sometimes with a little grass.
Nest site In a rabbit burrow, or sometimes under bushes or rocks.
Eggs 8–10, cream-coloured. 1 brood.
Incubation 29–31 days
First flight Leaves nest soon after hatching and flies after 45–50 days.
Food Snails and shrimp.

Duckling with down

COAST AND ESTUARY BIRDS

Oystercatcher
Haematopus ostralegus

Appearance Black and white with a long orange beak and pink legs.
Habits Mainly around coasts on rocks, beaches, and estuaries, but sometimes found on inland fields and shingle banks of rivers. Often noisy, it usually flies low with shallow wing-beats. Found in large flocks in autumn and winter.
Status Resident and winter visitor.
Size 43 cm (17 in)
Weight 400–700 g (14 oz–1½ lb)
Call A loud 'klee-eep, klee-eep' which can turn into a noisy, piping trill.
Nest Sometimes uses pieces of dead vegetation.
Nest site On the ground on shingle, rocks, or grass.
Eggs 3, yellowish or grey-buff with dark spots. 1 brood.
Incubation 24–27 days
First flight Leaves the nest a few hours after hatching and flies after 35–40 days.
Food Shellfish, crabs, worms, and insects.

Distinctive markings in flight

Oystercatcher

Ringed plover

Ringed Plover
Charadrius hiaticula

Appearance A small, brown plover with a clear black breast band and a black mask with a white forehead. The legs and beak are orange.

Black-tipped orange beak

Habits Found on sand and shingle coasts, estuaries, and sometimes at gravel pits inland. Runs rapidly for short distances, holding its head up. Tilts body when feeding. Flight is low and rapid. Feeds alone or in small groups.
Status Resident, passage migrant, and winter visitor.
Size 19 cm (7½ in)
Weight 55–75 g (2–2½ oz)
Call A melodious 'too-i'.
Nest Lined with stones and shells and occasionally vegetation.
Nest site On the ground in a hollow, usually on shingle, sand, or grass.
Eggs 4, grey to brown-buff, speckled with black. 1 brood.
Incubation 24–25 days
First flight Leaves nest soon after hatching and flies after 24 days.
Food Shellfish, insects, and worms.

87

COAST AND ESTUARY BIRDS

SANDERLING
Calidris alba

Appearance A small, white-looking wader with black legs and a black beak. Has a broad white wing bar that is visible in flight.

Foot with no hind toe

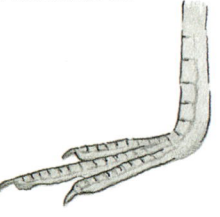

Habits Very active, running along the sand at the tide's edge, darting after food. Often quite tame. Usually found in small groups.
Status Passage migrant and winter visitor.
Size 20 cm (8 in)
Weight 45–85 g (1½–3 oz)
Call A shrill 'twick, twick' usually made when flying.
Nest A depression lined with leaves.
Nest site In a hollow on stony ground.
Eggs 4, olive green with dark blotches. 1 brood.
Incubation 24–27 days
First flight Leaves nest soon after hatching and flies after 23 or 24 days.
Food Sand-hoppers, shellfish, worms, and some insects.

DUNLIN
Calidris alpina

Appearance A brown wader with fairly long, slightly down-curved beak. The adult has a chestnut back and a black patch on its belly in summer.
Habits Found on upland grass moors in breeding season. Otherwise it likes muddy or sandy coasts and estuaries, as well as inland reservoirs and lakes.
Status Resident, passage migrant, and winter visitor.

Beaks come in differing sizes

Tail pattern in flight

Size 18 cm (7 in)
Weight 40–50 g (1½–1¾ oz)
Song A purring trill.
Call A shrill 'dzeep' usually made when flying.
Nest A shallow cup lined with grass or leaves.
Nest site In a clump of grass or heather.
Eggs 4, green or brown with dark blotches. 1 brood.
Incubation 21–22 days
First flight Leaves the nest almost immediately and flies after 19–21 days.
Food Insects, snails, and worms.

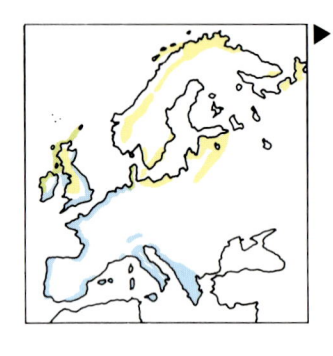

Dunlin

Sanderling

88

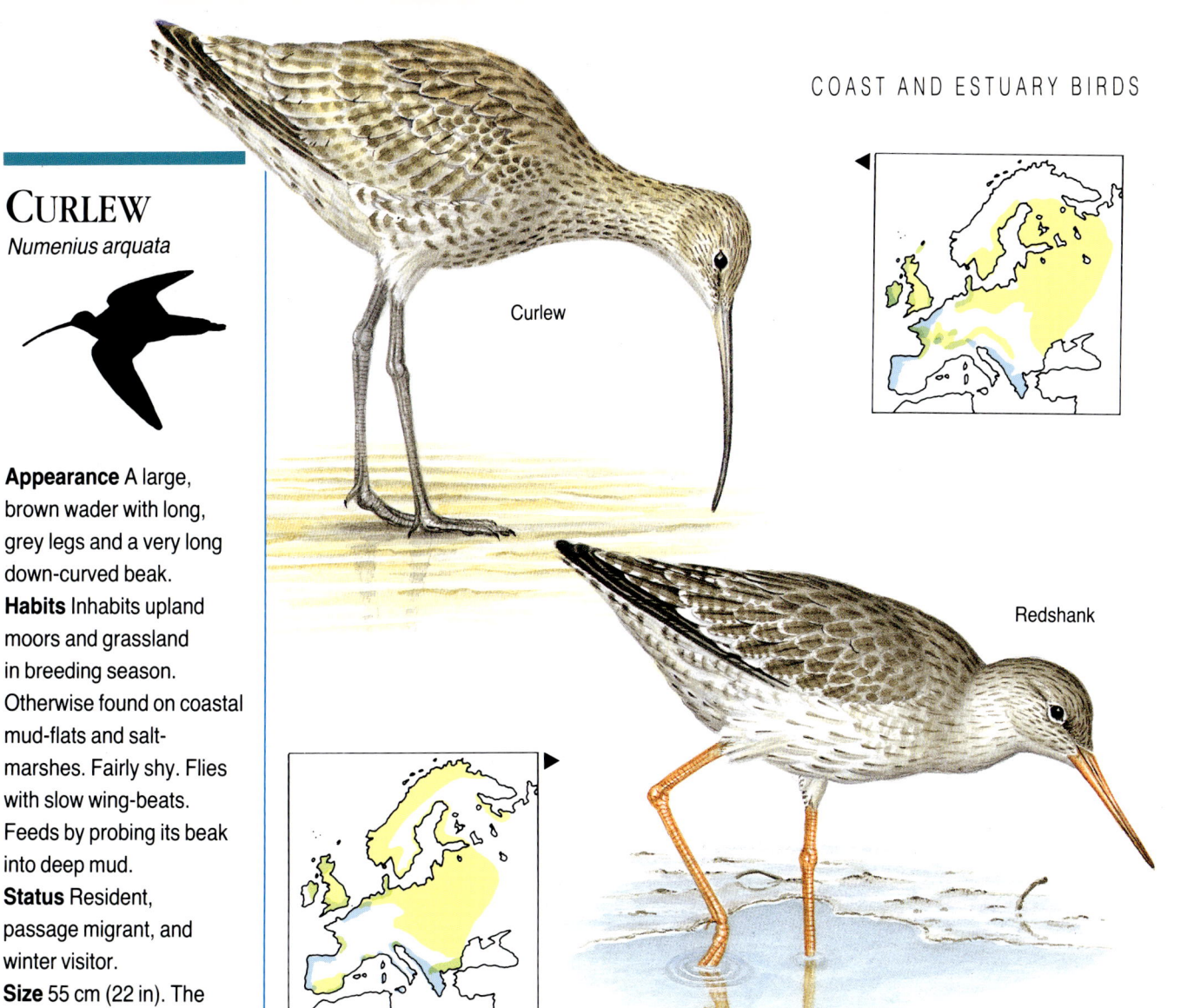

COAST AND ESTUARY BIRDS

Curlew
Numenius arquata

Appearance A large, brown wader with long, grey legs and a very long down-curved beak.
Habits Inhabits upland moors and grassland in breeding season. Otherwise found on coastal mud-flats and salt-marshes. Fairly shy. Flies with slow wing-beats. Feeds by probing its beak into deep mud.
Status Resident, passage migrant, and winter visitor.
Size 55 cm (22 in). The beak is about 12.5 cm (5 in).
Weight 575–800 g (1¼–1¾ lb)
Song A bubbling trill.
Call A characteristic 'coorlea'.
Nest A hollow lined with grasses.
Nest site On the ground among heather or grass.
Eggs 4, green or brown with dark spots. 1 brood.
Incubation 27–29 days
First flight Leaves the nest immediately and flies after 32–38 days.
Food Snails, shrimps, and worms.

White rump

Curlew

Redshank
Tringa totanus

Appearance A medium-sized brown wader with long orange-red legs and a long beak. Has white wing patches and a white rump that can be seen clearly in flight.
Habits Active and often noisy. Found at estuaries, mud-flats, and rocky shores, as well as inland lakes and marshes. Flies strongly and usually calls when disturbed.
Status Resident, passage migrant, and winter visitor.

Typical perching position

Redshank

Size 28 cm (11¼ in)
Weight 110–155 g (4–5½ oz)
Song A trilling and yodelling 'tu-udle, tu-udle'.
Call A loud 'tiuu-huu-huu' or short 'tiuu'.
Nest In a hollow lined with dry grass.
Nest site In a clump of long grass in wet meadow or marsh.
Eggs 4, creamy buff with dark blotches. 1 brood.
Incubation 22–24 days
First flight Leaves the nest soon after hatching and flies after 25–35 days.
Food Insects, snails, and worms.

GLOSSARY

A

Aves The animal class, or group, to which all birds belong.

B

Barb A small horizontal 'branch' from the central shaft of a feather. Neighbouring barbs join to form the feather's surface.
Bracken A plant found on heathland. It is related to ferns.
Bramble The blackberry bush. This is a thorny bush which many birds like to nest in.
Brood The young hatched from a single clutch, or group, of eggs.

C

Call Any sound made by a bird which is not a song.
Carrion A dead animal. Scavengers eat these.
Clutch A single group of eggs laid in a nest.
Colony A group of birds which nests closely together. Rooks often form colonies.
Copse A small group of trees.
Covey A group of partridges. It often consists of parents with their young.
Courtship The activity which leads to the pairing of a male and female bird before breeding. Courtship often involves song and display.
Crustaceans Small freshwater or seawater animals, such as shrimps, sand-hoppers, and water fleas, which are eaten by many birds.

D

Display Behaviour that a male bird uses to attract a female partner. It often involves song, calls, and showing bright feathers. Other displays are also used when two birds fight over a territory.
Down The small, soft feathers which cover very young birds. Down also covers the skin of adult birds underneath their body feathers, keeping them warm.

E

Egg tooth A small sharp 'hook' at the tip of a young bird's beak. This enables the bird to break out of its egg. This tip breaks off while hatching.
Estuary The wide mouth of a river. An estuary includes sand, mudflats, and any plants at the edges.
Evolution The process by which animals and plants have gradually changed over a long period of time. They change to take the best advantage of their surroundings and ensure their survival.
Excavate To dig out a nesting chamber. Woodpeckers, for example, excavate trees, while kingfishers excavate in a bank.

F

Family A group of one or more closely related bird species. Members of a family sometimes belong to different genera.
Fledgling A young bird which has only just flown from its nest.

G

Genus/genera A group of one or more closely related bird species. The name of a genus forms the first part of a bird's scientific name. Genera is the plural of genus.
Gorse A prickly plant with yellow flowers that forms dense bushes on heathland. It is used by many birds as a nest site.

H

Habitat The kind of place where an animal or plant lives. Woodland, estuaries, and marshes are examples of habitats.
Heath A habitat that usually includes plants such as heather and gorse, with scattered trees and bushes.
Heather A small, bushy plant, usually found covering heathland and moorland. It often has pink or purple flowers.
Hummock A small hill or raised area of ground.

I

Incubate To sit on eggs to keep them warm while the chicks grow inside.

Instinct A natural action which has not been learned. A duckling swimming for the first time is an example.

L

Lobe A flap of skin which some water birds, such as the crested grebe and coot, have along the edges of their toes. Lobes help birds to swim.

M

Marsh A habitat made up of a very wet area of grass or other plants.
Mate One of a pair of birds. Also refers to the joining together of a male and female to reproduce.
Migrant A bird which breeds in one area and flies some distance to a different area to spend the winter. Many migrants travel vast distances. This is known as migration.
Moor A habitat found in hilly areas with mainly heather and no trees. It is often damp or boggy.
Moult To lose old feathers and grow new ones. Most birds replace their feathers once a year after the breeding season. Some birds replace some of their feathers at other times.
Mudflat A flat area of mud found at the edge of an estuary. It is usually covered at high tide. A mudflat is a favourite area for waders to feed.

N
Nest Where a bird lays its eggs. A nest can be a complicated structure of twigs and grass, or a simple hollow on the ground.
Nestbox A box put up as an artificial nesting place for some birds.

O
Order A group of one or more related bird families (eg ducks, geese, and swans).
Ornithology The study of birds and their behaviour.

P
Passage migrant A migrant bird which passes through an area between its breeding and wintering areas.
Passeriformes A large order of birds which contains all of the perching birds. These are often small birds and all of them sing as part of their courtship.
Plumage The covering of feathers on a bird's body.
Predator An animal which eats other animals, catching them alive.

R
Resident A bird species which can be found in a particular area throughout the year.
Rookery A large group of rooks' nests. Also called a colony.
Roost A place where birds sleep. Some birds, such as owls, roost during the daytime, others, such as waders, at high tide.

S
Saltmarsh The muddy area, covered with plants, at the edge of an estuary or coast.
Sand-hopper A small crustacean found on the seashore. Many coastal birds feed on sand-hoppers.
Scavenger A bird which eats scraps and carrion.
Shaft The stiff, central part of a feather. This is what gives the feather its strength.
Song The complicated sounds produced by many species of birds, usually males. Song is used to attract mates and mark out a territory.
Song flight A special display by some bird species. The male sings while flying to attract a mate or mark out a territory.
Song perch A favourite place used by a male bird when marking out its territory.
Species A type of bird which has a common name, such as jackdaw, and a scientific name, such as *Corvus monedula*. The last part of the scientific name identifies the species, the first part identifies the genus.
Status A description of how common a bird is and whether it is a resident, migrant, or passage migrant.

T
Territory The area which a pair of birds use to raise their young. Any other birds of the same species are kept out of the territory.

U
Undergrowth Low plants which grow underneath trees and bushes.

W
Wader A member of a group of related birds, many of which are found wading in estuaries, coastal areas or marshes. Examples are the dunlin, oystercatcher, and curlew.
Wildfowl A general name given to groups of ducks, geese, and swans.

HELPFUL ORGANIZATIONS

Young Ornithologists' Club (junior branch of the Royal Society for the Protection of Birds), The Lodge, Sandy, Bedfordshire SG19 2DL.

WATCH (junior branch of the Royal Society for Nature Conservation), The Green, Witham Park, Waterside South, Lincoln LN5 7JR.

British Trust for Ornithology, The Nunnery, Nunnery Place, Thetford, Norfolk IP24 2PU.

INDEX

Note: page numbers in *italic* refer to illustrations

A

Arctic tern, migration *24*, 25

B

beaks 18, 82
binoculars 12–13, *12*
bird calls 43
bird names 26, 27
bird song *13*, 43
bird tables 28, 29
birds
  appearance 27
  behaviour 14, 20–1
  bodies 16–19
  habits 27
  identification *10*, 11, 14, 26–7
  life cycles 22–3
  plumage 16–18, *16*, *17*
birds of prey 56
  beaks 18
  feet 19
  sight 56
birdwatching 10, 11, 28, *40*, 54, *68*, 80
  making notes 14–15
  safety 80
  time of year 11–12
black-headed gull 76, *76*
blackbird 11, 14, 35, *35*
  chicks 22
  food 29
  nest 22
  territory 21
blackcap *41*, 48, *48*
blue tit 36, *36*
  eggs *22*
  nesting places 23
breeding 21, 22–3
bullfinch 53, *53*
  food 42
  nesting place 23
bunting 40
buzzard 56, 58, *58*
  food 55
  talons *19*, *58*

C

call notes 20, 27
Canada goose *10*, 11, 73, *73*
carrion crow 65, *65*
chaffinch 11, 39, *39*
  nesting place 23
chick types 22
chiffchaff 47, *47*
  habitat *41*
  migration *24*
  nesting place 23
  song 43
coal tit 51, *51*
  habitat 43
  nesting place 23
coast birds 80–9
coastal areas 12
collared dove 32, *32*
common tern 76, *76*
  feeding 69–70
coot 71, 75, *75*
diving 70
feet *19*, 69
fighting *21*
cormorant *18*, 83, 84, *84*
food 80
Corvidae 26
courtship displays 20
crow family 26
cuckoo 14, 61, *61*
  nesting 57, *57*
  song 20
curlew 89, *89*
  beaks 82
  food *83*
  habitat 57, 81

D

dipper 77, *77*
display flights 20
down feathers 16–17
ducks *19*, *19*, 69, 74
dunlin 88, *88*
  beak 82, *88*
  food *83*
  habitat 14, 81
  migration 25
  roosts 13
dunnock 38, *38*
  feeding cuckoo *61*

E

eagle, talons *19*
egg tooth 23
eggs *22*, 23, 27
  incubation 23, 27, 31, *31*
estuaries 81

F

farming methods 54–5
feathers 13, *13*, 15, 16–18, *16*
  moulting 17
  preening 13
feeders 29, 30
feeding *10*, 13, 30
feeding levels 70
feet 19, *19*, 69
feral pigeon 32, *32*
field guides 15
fieldfare 64, *64*
  food 29
  migration 25, 54
finches 39, 40, 53, 66
  beak 18
  food 42
  roost 43
flight 14, 17, 18, 27
flocks 14, 55–6, *55*

migrating *24*
food 27, *29*

G

garden birds 28–40
garden warbler 48, *48*
geese 73
  feet 19, 69
  habitat 12
  migration *24*
goldcrest 40, 49
  call 43
  courtship display 20, *21*
  habitat *41*, 43
  nesting place 23
golden plover 60, *60*
  flocks 56
  habitat 57
goldfinch *15*, 57, 66, *66*
  food 31
great crested grebe 71, 72, *72*
  courtship display 20
  diving 70
  feet 69, *72*
  nest 71
great spotted woodpecker 23, 46, *46*
great tit 11, 36, *36*
green woodpecker 43, 46, *46*
greenfinch *18*, 39, *39*
  food 29
grey heron 72, 83, *72*
  food 70, 71, *71*
  nest 71
grey partridge 57, 59, *59*
gulls 76, 85
  feet 19, 69
  food *81*
  migration *24*

H

herring gull 85, *85*
  feet *19*, 85
  food 80, *81*
  nesting site 83
hides 14
hooded crow 65
house martin 33, *33*
  breeding 31
  food 70
  migration *24*
house sparrow 14, 38, *38*
  nest 71

I

identification of birds 14
insect-eating birds 70–1

J

jackdaw 14, 37, *37*
  name 26
  walk 14
jay *14*, 26, 50, *50*
  food 41, *42*
  hopping 14

K

kestrel 14, *19*, 56, 57, 58, *58*
  beak *18*, *58*
  food 55
  nests 31, 57
kingfisher 71, 77, *77*, 83
  feet 77
  food 70, 71
kittiwake 85, *85*
  feet *85*
  food 80
  nesting site *21*, 83

L

lake birds 68–79
lapwing 57, 60, *60*

chicks 22
flocks 56
nest 23
Latin names 26, 27
linnet 67, 67
   food 31
   habitat 57
long-tailed tit 11, 50, 50
   nest 23
   tail feather 50

M

magpie 26, 66, 66
mallard 11, 68, 74, 74
   beak 18
marsh birds 68–79
marsh tit 51, 51
meadow pipit 57, 63, 63
migration 12, 24–5
   passage migrants 25, 27
   routes 24
moorhen 71, 75, 75
moulting 17
mute swan 14, 73, 73
   diving 70
   feeding 70, 73
   feet 19, 69
   mating dance 20
   nest 71
   number of feathers 17–18

N

nest boxes 30, 30
nest sites 13, 22, 27
nest types 22
nests
   building 13
   woodland 43
note taking 14, 15
nuthatch 29, 40, 40, 52, 52
   nest site 43

O

oil hazard 82
open countryside birds 54–67
owls 44, 56, 61
oystercatcher 18, 87, 87
   eggs 82

P

passage migrants 25, 27
Passeriformes 26
pheasant 14, 19, 59
   feathers 18, 59
   nest 22
photographing birds 42
pied wagtail 11, 14, 56, 63, 63
   roost 55
pigeons 32, 45, 57
plant food for birds 31
plumage *see* feathers
pond dipping 70
puffin 83, 84, 84
   eggs 22, 23
   food 80

R

racing pigeon 32
redshank 83, 89, 89
   habitat 81
redstart, nest site 43
redwing 12, 64, 64
   flocks 54
   food 29
   migration 25, 25
reed bunting 40, 79, 79
reed warbler 68, 71, 78, 78
   cuckoo's nest 57
resident birds 27
ringed plover 87, 87
   eggs 82, 82
   food 83

river birds 68–79
robin 34, 34
   feet 19
   food 29
   nest 23
   nesting box 30
   song 20
   territory 20, 21
rock dove 32, 32
rook 65, 65
   nesting places 57
roosting 13, 55

S

safety 80
sanderling 82, 88, 88
   migration 25
scientific names 26, 27
seabirds 80–9
seasonal visitors 24–5
sedge warbler 71, 71, 78, 78
   display flights 20, 21
shelduck 81, 86, 86
short-eared owl 56, 61, 61
   territory 21
siskin 53, 53
   food 42
   habitat 41, 43
   nesting place 23
skylark 57, 62, 62
   display flights 20, 21
   egg incubation 23
song 27
song thrush 35, 35
sparrow hawk 44, 44
   food 31, 43
spotted flycatcher 18, 41, 49
starling 11, 14, 37, 37
   food 29

roost 30, 43
run 14
swallow 11, 12, 56, 62, 62
   eggs 31
   food 70
   migration 24
   nest 31
swan *see* mute swan
swift 11, 33, 33
   beak 18, 33
   breeding 31
   feet 19, 33

T

tails 18, 18
tawny owl 44, 44
   habitat 41
terns 76, 82
territory 21
thrush
   food 29
   roost 43
tits 36, 40, 50, 51
   food 29, 31, 42
   nest sites 43
   nesting boxes 30
town birds 28–40
treecreeper 40, 41, 52, 52
   song 43
tufted duck 69, 74
   diet 70
turtle dove 45, 45
   nesting place 23

U

underwater food 70
uplands birds 54–67

V

visitors 27

W

waders 12, 18, 80, 81, 82

wagtails 63, 70, 79
warblers 47, 48, 70, 78
water birds 19, 69
water sources 28
wetlands 12, 68
white wagtail 63
wigeon 81, 86, 86
   migration 24
wildfowl 69, 80, 81
willow warbler 47, 47
   habitat 41
   migration 24, 25
   nesting place 23
wings 16, 18, 19, 19
woodland birds 40–53
woodpecker 14, 19, 46
woodpigeon 14, 41, 45, 45
   eggs 42
   feeding 31
   habitat 41
   nesting place 23, 42
   song 43
wren 14, 27, 27, 34, 34

Y

yellow hammer 57, 67, 67
yellow wagtail 79, 79
   food 70
Young Ornithologists Club 11

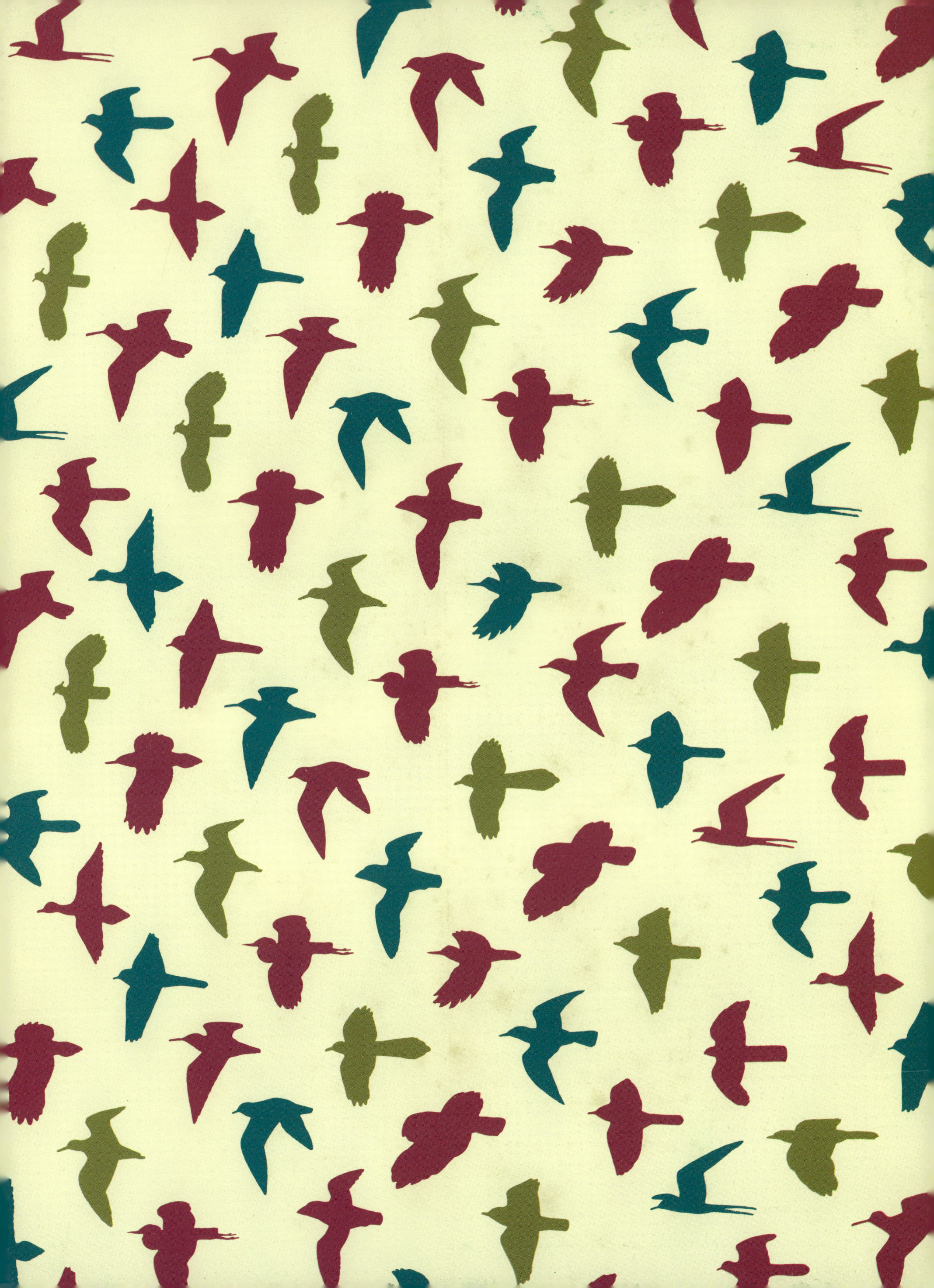